In The Midst of Darkness

A "Schindler's List" Survivor's Story Never Told

Robert Don

Table of Contents

Rosa Laufer Don
My Mother.

Kathy Baetka Don
My Stepmother.

Morris Don
My Father near downtown
Berlin during summer, 1948.

Robert Don –
I was 4 1/2 years old.

Harry and Mindel Don
My brother's Bar Mitzvah celebration,
being with my father's mother.

All photos: © Robert Don

Preface

Growing up, both my brother Harry and I never really had our own lens for how we perceived our father and particularly our German stepmother (Kathy). Our deep, bitter hatred for our stepmother was seen through our mother's eyes. The hatred was sometimes manifested by my brother violently. These perceptions were due to our mother's trauma from the Holocaust that became our trauma.

How can racism begin? We have to first understand how it's defined – assumptions of people based upon stereotypes. Can it begin when you're being told what to believe as a child and you really don't know any better? Is there any deeper impact than to children, whose minds are shaped by authority figures – parents in this context - that infiltrate their kids' minds with false beliefs? I was that child learning to hate. It's what my mother told me to do. While deeply sad, it was normal behavior. I don't know what's worse, knowing that deep hatred existed, or knowing I couldn't change anything. The irony being that I was a perpetrator of hatred, while after many years of not understanding why, I was a victim of hatred – my mother's.

There has been much shared of survivors' accounts of the atrocities they lived through in the Holocaust, but not nearly enough of the impact of their trauma upon their children. This is what my brother and I grew up with as children; our mother's trauma being our trauma.

The reach of darkness for the memories first told to my brother – Harry and I as children leads to understanding why we were deeply impacted by "Second Generation" holocaust survivor trauma. My mother inflicted her bitter hatred for my stepmother on both of us. We lived with our perceptions being her perceptions. There is no opportunity for change when the relentless hatred you feel begins when you're a child. We were just that vulnerable, having nothing else to draw upon that may have changed how we felt. That's what we knew.

The tragedy maybe even wasn't my mother's trauma, which manifested into the deep hatred that had penetrated too far inside me, but in what I didn't know and why. If I had known what my mother never told me, there could have been hope I would have grown up differently. Our memories of inconceivable trauma never really leave us and anything positive which can insulate you from the pain may be only temporarily forgotten or not able to change you. But there was something I felt that probably re-triggered my mother's darkness about the Holocaust and all that she lost, nearly two decades later. It buried what she knew and I should have known. Maybe that's what happened to my mother.

Her darkness and vengeance that lived within me since I was a child has left me compelled to tell why I was that helpless. That I was only a child being defenseless to know differently pushes me to begin with the most traumatic memories growing up. I couldn't change my perceptions of my stepmother and all Germans, but how I grew up lets me know why.

CHAPTER I

Growing Up – Memories of Deep Hatred and What I Didn't Know

My mother first told me she was a Holocaust survivor when I was five years old. She told me that at first with no emotion. However, shortly thereafter, probably remembering what happened to her, she couldn't hide from the scale of darkness within her past. It was more deep anger than despair I saw in her face of suffering for no reason, and what was taken from her and never returned. Losses that no one could ever understand or replace.

How much of what happened to her had to really matter, being something that would come to traumatically define her life?. She lost her parents, four sisters and a brother in the Belzec and Auschwitz death camps, all murdered in the gas chambers. The family lost their home, three businesses and their money – their assets would have totaled over $1 million today, and it was all confiscated by the Nazis during Adolf Hitler's reign of terror.

She survived the Holocaust only because of the actions of an Austrian businessman, who was a member of the Nazi Party – because of Oskar Schindler. But I never knew that she was on Schindler's list, not until 1993 – five years after she died. I never knew why she didn't tell me – and I've accepted that I never will.

Schindler was born in Austria like Hitler and while they were not of pure German ethnicity they were still considered Nazi Germans. The Nazis defined "German" through their racist Aryan ideology, persecuting Jews, Roma ("Gypsies) and Slavs, while recruiting many non-Germans into their military.

Since the time my mother revealed she had been a Holocaust survivor, when I was only a child, she had deeply influenced me to see Germans as different than other people. From early childhood, I was taught to see Germans as persecutors, as the evil who destroyed my mother's family – visualizing the horror that my mother and every other Jew faced in the concentration camps. It was as if she wanted me to share her fear, her hatred, no matter how afraid it made me. As a child, I couldn't comprehend her pain – being alone just six months after turning 16, no parents, no sisters or her brother, and living with the memories of what was taken from her. As she reflected on her past, an overwhelming anger crept into her voice. I knew that when I saw that image across her face of what she lived through in the Holocaust, she was trapped in the past – living in the memories of what was taken from her.

Any hope my mother had of overcoming her deep hatred toward German people ended when my father separated from my mother, leaving her for Kathy. Her full name was Kathy Baetka. She was German and nothing about her was Jewish. Even my mother knowing that Kathy was with a Jewish man couldn't change the fact that she thought that all Germans were disgusted by Jews. But how could Kathy have been with a Jewish man, if all Germans hated Jews? I guess my mother hated them all. No one could have felt deeper betrayal than she did – knowing my father left her for a German woman after what happened to her in the Holocaust.

I am certain part of what he was taken by in Kathy was excitement, knowing my father's unconforming ways. He rebelled against a marriage and a Jewish tradition that was forced upon him for all the wrong reasons after the Holocaust to be with a German. My father left in the winter of 1962 when my mother was eight months pregnant with me. She couldn't stop him from leaving, despite all the guilt she wanted him to feel before he left. I know that what happened and my mother having loved my father as much as she did, destroyed what was left of her after the Holocaust. Since that day, she would only refer to Kathy as the "Shiksa" and "Deichke." These are derogatory names in Yiddish that Jewish people have for non-Jewish women.

But my parents' marriage wasn't the story of two people who fell in and out of love – my grandmother (Mindel) was the one who strongly encouraged or more forced my father to marry my mother. My parents were living in Berlin, having moved there separately from the DP (Displaced Persons) camps in 1947 after the concentration camps were liberated in 1945. They were waiting to come to America, once the borders began to open in mid-1948, and they met in early 1949. My mother became pregnant with my brother that next year while they were dating in Berlin. My grandmother thought due to my mother being Jewish, now pregnant, and seeing my father often being more of a child than an adult, marriage would give them Jewish children and some very needed grounding for him. Mindel was a strong-minded woman and Judaism and family were everything to her.

I've felt particularly later in life as an adult looking back on my mother and father's relationship that he had been trapped in a marriage which never should have happened. But more importantly, who was to blame? Was it my mother, who my father blamed, since she loved him that much and didn't want him to leave? Or was it really my grandmother, who I felt forced him into something that he never wanted to do? But despite what probably happened, he held it against my mother that she'd pushed him to be with her against his will. My father could never blame his mother for what she did to him. He loved her way too much.

There were many arranged and nearly arranged marriages of Jewish people after the concentration camps were liberated, due to some survivors who felt the only way to prevent another Jewish genocide was to procreate. That didn't work out well for my mother and father's marriage, having a relationship that was really never based upon mutual love from what I know. My mother deeply loved my father, but it wasn't reciprocal.

In the 10 years they were married, my father didn't express much love, or any real affection for my mother. Often being toxic and losing restraint, he could become emotionally hostile to her and she defensive to him. She wanted a family, and he would refuse – either not wanting to have one or not with her. That, I believe is what pushed him over the edge, feeling he was forced to have a family with her.

My stepmother once said when I was in my 30's that my father would have had a family with her. But he believed that having other children would deeply hurt my brother and I – maybe knowing we were traumatically impacted when he left my mother being pregnant for another woman. That alone would have been enough, but there might have been far more guilt that he left her for a German woman. I never asked my father whether what Kathy had told me was true. I was afraid that I wouldn't believe him, if he agreed with what she said.

I often felt that way when I was older because my father grew up differently than my mother. Maybe he just didn't want to have kids.

My mother also told me she had four miscarriages while married to my father. She mentioned that more than a few times, covered in tears. It was due to my father screaming at her with that much contempt each time she was pregnant, "I don't want to have children." The stress caused her to miscarry. It was nearly a miracle my brother and I were conceived. During her pregnancy with me, his rage at having another child almost caused her to lose me at least twice before birth.

The differences between my mother and father were always that clear. She was from the old country in Krakow (Poland) – came from a very traditional and Orthodox family. He was from Warsaw, Poland, not religious, very adventurous and wild, never really willing to be domesticated. He drank heavily, loved to be out at night, and was very promiscuous. He told me when I was older that while incarcerated within a Siberian Labor camp during the war, he and some of the prisoners would steal vodka off the trucks that came to the labor camp for the soldiers and sell it back to them, just so he could have money to pay off people in the camp for his own booze. My father didn't have fear; that's how he survived the camps. Despite failing in five businesses when he came to the US, it didn't stop him. He became an entrepreneurial success in his sixth venture in the automobile business.

Kathy in nearly every way was a deep contrast to my mother – blond hair, blue eyes, always elegantly dressed and attractive, meticulous to a model that maybe no one was like and religion didn't matter much to her. My father met her when he went to Germany to visit his brother Schmilky (Sam in English), who owned a bar–restaurant in Berlin.

She was a waitress, and they met one night while my father was having dinner in his brother's pub. German music was playing and the laughter of patrons filled the air. He was far away from a pregnant wife, a 10-year-old son and a little 2-room apartment. He was taken by Kathy right from the moment they met, stunned with her blond hair, blue eyes and fair complexion.

My mother's physical appearance was heavily, darkly accentuated. Her eyes were deep, dark brown, with defining bold black hair and a profoundly dark colored complexion, often distinctive features of Jewish people. While my mother was an attractive woman, she was much shorter than my stepmother, dressed traditionally as if she still lived in the old country, and her hygiene and broader cleanliness were not priorities. This was deeply apparent living in a home that was often filthy – never being very well kept.

My parents were maybe well suited for each other, but only when considering their backgrounds (both were Jewish and Holocaust survivors); Otherwise they lived in different worlds. The costs from the carnage of their marriage included the losses that I sustained, growing up feeling some of the deep betrayal that my mother felt from my father when he left her and the hostility towards him for leaving. That damage and uncontrollable hatred which, my mother also inflicted in my brother towards Kathy critically impacted him. He was left with suffering he didn't deserve that could never be measured. His crisis became his fate.

People may have certain backgrounds, such as my parents, and maybe that's enough as to why some may feel two people are right for each other. But that's not always what's right for the couple. Also, people who grow up differently are not always wrong for each other. Our differences define us, but much too often aren't valued enough in relationships. They weren't reconcilable in my parents' marriage.

Given no choice but to breathe my mother's trauma, I had to grow up through her victim's lens of the Holocaust. She couldn't get through the past and all that was lost. Her stories and her priorities always reflected the past, and she taught me to see the world this way, from the moment I was old enough to listen to the memories she shared with me. These were the prejudices I, too, began to form – not knowing the one part of her history she never told me.

I had the right to know that not all Germans were Nazis, who condoned the dehumanization of people – primarily those who were Jewish. Schindler himself showed a depth of conviction to humanity, which isolated him from the rest of the fascist party's ideological ambition – saving and not murdering Jewish people, despite the stench of bitter Jewish hatred that penetrated across Europe.

My mother's deep and a near lifetime of unrelenting bitterness toward all Germans easily penetrated me by what she once told me as a child. Still, it was assumptions about every German that manifested as nothing more than her own bias.

"The Germans that lived next to Jews had no feelings and didn't want to know what was happening in the Holocaust." She told me that with a bitter, cold, nasty, chilling face. She'd go on for hours, making sure I was deeply exposed to every bit of what she had gone through.

"If you only knew what the Nazis did to us and how all Germans were complicit or indifferent to what was being done to us. The German people knew the Nazis came on trucks in the middle of the night to round up Jews."

"It was so no one could see them bringing them to the ghettos. Then we were no more use to them or the ghettos were liquidated, were deported tothe camps. Jews were taken from nearly every European country - Poland, Germany, Czechoslovakia, Romania, Hungary, France and Holland."

"They knew Jews were being beaten, starved and murdered in ways no one could believe."

I was filled with fear and rage every time I heard these stories. How could these people have done this to my mother and her family? They were all victims and no one could help them. At the time, I came to think like her because I thought I was defending her. How could I know there were righteous amongst the mass of evil, those who didn't conform to or weren't complicit in the Nazis' atrocities? No one ever told me about the ones in the Holocaust who lived with the unrelenting commitment for people to be treated like themselves – as people.

It's possible that maybe even only a few years after the Holocaust, my mother was no longer conscious of what Schindler did for her, or to what scale he'd saved so many Jewish lives. I blame that on the gravity of her losses the Nazis inflicted and years later my father leaving her for a German woman.

As I was growing up, my mother's stories of the history and dehumanization of Jews during the Holocaust left me with deep hatred for all Germans, and that included my stepmother. Her hatred for Kathy and every other German were a mirror for my beliefs. I was so angry with the world on her behalf. How could such hate and cruelty exist? The stories I heard couldn't leave me feeling any differently. I was a child and had nothing else to draw upon, other than what she told me.

I remember that my mother used to frequently walk around the house naked. I was maybe 9 or 10 and became so embarrassed to see her standing in front of the living room window not wearing anything. I sometimes closed my eyes with heavy fear, just hoping that none of my friends would be walking by during those moments. I didn't know what do; I didn't know whether to demand that she dress herself, or stay as far away as possible during these times. That feeling of internal conflict is one with which I'd grow to become familiar. I did often ask her why she wasn't dressed.

"Mom, don't you care what people who see you could say and what they'll think of us?"

She responded by saying:

"Once we arrived in Auschwitz, they unloaded the prisoners from the cattle cars, and we were then separated into groups – men, and women and children. One of the Nazi doctors would look at us and determine if we were sick, or too young to work."

"After the doctor's examination, they would point to two lines. If their hand pointed in one direction, you were in the line for forced laborers. If the hand pointed the other way, you would not return – you were being led to the gas chambers."

"I was in the line for forced laborers. We were registered, given a prison number and then told to take off all our clothes. They shaved our heads to remove any lice and we were forced to shower to help eliminate diseases the doctors believed we had."

"We stripped naked usually in front of hundreds of other people, as well as the SS Guards. Not wearing clothes just seems normal, given what sometimes happened when I was in the Plaszow concentration camp ("Plaszow") for selection of deportation to a death camp."

"That's what also happened when I came to Auschwitz."

The humiliating process for forced laborers was designed by the Nazis to remove any human dignity or personal identity from the prisoners. My mother wouldn't stop crying when she talked about the doctor's hand, if it pointed to the other line that wasn't for forced labor, as she remembered how her parents, sisters and a brother that died in the gas chambers. Her tears didn't stop, knowing that line was also the fate for so many others entering Auschwitz and the Belzec extermination camps.

When I heard her story, I was overwhelmed by the past in the way that she wanted me to be. What my mother had been through was inconceivable. This was one of various ways she reacted to her trauma in Plaszow and Auschwitz – deep memories of tormenting, repeated darkness that manifested through her perception of normal behavior.

The way she walked around the house naked had to be reflexive for how she lived in the camps. And given her past, I knew it was important to be compassionate, thankful for her and that she survived.

But at the same time, I was still deeply embarrassed and very disgusted, crushed by shame, particularly when the kids on my block actually saw her like that in front of the window. They would sometimes line up on the sidewalk, looking into the living room window like watching a strip or porn show. They made sure to keep their distance, so she wouldn't be able to see them very easily. They would sometimes refer to it as "The Operation." Kids can be so evil, putting others in such a compromised position. And I couldn't do anything about it.

The memories of what she lived through in the Holocaust only made her hatred for my stepmother come that much easier. I also couldn't be more vulnerable as a child being left with her perceptions.

One of the earliest times that I remembered the hatred my mother had for Kathy was a bike accident when I was five. What happened back then was responsible for how I began to hate my stepmother. It never left me when I was older and even when I became an adult.

I crashed on a bike and hit my forehead on a concrete step of an apartment building near my house. I remember flying down the street feeling so cool on my new bike that day, being a kid growing up. Then, all of a sudden, I was on the ground, my blood staining the concrete steps and my bike's frame cracked in at least two or three places. One of my friends who was with me rushed to my house and told my mother about the accident.

She and my father ran over and looked at me lying in a pool of blood, and my injuries required 15 stitches to my forehead. To this day, there is still a scar on my head due to the accident. I remember how my mother began yelling and crying hysterically to my father that day.

> "You bought him a German bike. You and your Deichke whore bought him a German bike. You left me for that bitch and your gift for his birthday was a German bike. She and her family lived among Nazis and they weren't any better than them."

"My family was murdered in Auschwitz and Belzec, and you know what I had to live through in the camps, yet you purchased Bobby a German bike. You're not his father."

I don't remember what he said back to my mother. It didn't matter. I was only five and couldn't separate myself from her perceptions. All I know is that my mother blamed my father for buying me the bike and I absorbed all the rage inside her for my father, not to mention my stepmother. It was so clear by what happened – you don't have a choice when you're that young, except to believe what your mother is telling you.

The memories of what my mother did to me, living with her vengeance for my stepmother since childhood, and the relationship with my father compromised by some intense hatred for him, left me deeply overwhelmed growing up. My mother was psychologically traumatized by the Holocaust, but I couldn't see past what she was doing to me. I was blinded by my own circumstances and felt almost claustrophobic when I tried to make sense of it all. I probably couldn't really understand the scale of her trauma. I only knew I was deeply impacted by her past.

She put me in charge from a young age of getting her $200 a week alimony check from my father when it wasn't mailed like it should have been. That was much too often. I would go to his office when I was maybe 9 or 10, he would take me out for lunch and get me a new toy, while I was forced to ask him for my mother's alimony check.

I always dreaded the moment I had to ask and nearly panicked every time, like it was a pill I couldn't swallow. The chilling fear was due to knowing he deeply resented me asking him for it. He would often show his rage – intended for my mother - when I asked him for the check. The blistering redness spread all over his face. He wasn't much less angry with me for asking him. I would ask myself, how could my mother do that to me? Didn't she know what that cost me, being put in the middle of their conflict? But I was just much too afraid confronting her as a child.

I guess that's what divorce can do; leave children in the middle with no way out. If our parents only knew how their children can become collateral damage, while in pursuit of their own selfish agendas.

I always believed my father got me what I wanted growing up to absolve his guilt for leaving my mother and marrying a German woman. He also wasn't around much and we usually only saw each other on the weekends, or going to see ball games and hockey games on a weekday occasionally. I was a very spoiled kid – always the best seats for games, eating at fancy restaurants with my father and he always bought me my favorite toys.

But I couldn't escape the lingering feeling that he was doing all of this because he felt like he had to, not because he wanted to. This may have even more deeply impacted him because he was living with Kathy in a Jewish neighborhood and had family friends who were European Jews. Many of them were Holocaust survivors in the concentration camps, those who'd been hiding, or on the run from the Nazis over that six year period of probably the darkest chapter in history.

How was my father really able to live with a German woman in one of Chicago's largest Jewish neighborhoods – Rogers Park being filled with Holocaust survivors in the 1960's and 70's? They had to have seen her as such a lethal enemy, a perpetrator, due to their own trauma, but maybe not to the extent of my mother. Shockingly, I don't know how, but to some extent my father assimilated Kathy into the Jewish community, with four or five couples who were survivors that were friends they played cards with weekly and went to dinner with sometimes. Somehow they had learned not do what my mother had done – hold every German accountable for the atrocities committed by those that did.

There were times growing up I was consumed with rage, knowing my father and Kathy had friends who were survivors. I just thought, how could these people, let alone my father – being survivors have lived with themselves and forgotten their past? They felt like very reasonable perceptions, considering I was that deeply manipulated – victimized by my mother's penetration of hatred.

When I came to his office a few times and saw Kathy there, I left immediately. I was overcome with a combination of fear, rage, and guilt that I was somehow betraying my mother. In a state of panic, with emotion that crowded all of my senses, I would rush out of his office, not even say goodbye, take the bus home and run four blocks from the bus station as fast as I could. Once home, I would seek the smothering affection of my mother. Or if I couldn't leave because my father had already seen me, I panicked and cried without end.

"How can you be with her? I can't stay. You married a Shiksa.
Do you know what her family must have done to my mother
and her family? They were Nazis. I can't stay. Please take
me home now. I will never see you when she's here. Never."

My father wouldn't say much when he answered. He had a guarded, broken expression as he tried to calm me down and take me home. It always really hurt him that I couldn't accept her as his wife, even if he kept that emotion buried inside. He wanted me to have a relationship with her, but how could I the way I was growing up? I knew my mother had done everything possible for me to see Kathy, as well as him only through her eyes.

I did love my father and considered him much "cooler" than my mother, the way he gave everything, knowing my mother wouldn't. He even let me drink part of his beer when I was 11 at a baseball game. My mother never really took me out to dinner; we were religious Jews and kept Kosher. I never liked Kosher food and really only went with her to services and social events in synagogues, or to her friends' houses who were Holocaust survivors, or was dragged to social outings by Jewish organizations for survivors. I often found it hard to express myself when I was with her by asking why we couldn't do other things. Everything had to be through her lens – living with the Holocaust.

When I was 12, I couldn't stop asking my father for a motorcross bike, which he finally bought me. My mother begged him not to way too many times, being certain I would get into an accident and badly hurt. When he purchased the bike, he mentioned that if he ever visited me in the hospital due to an accident, he'd take it away instantly. That finally came true when I crashed into a car pulling out of an alley. I wound up in the hospital with 25 stitches in my ankle (scars to this day which never healed) and when he came to my room he didn't say more than a few words.

"You remember what I said? When you leave the hospital,
I'll get someone to pick up the motorcycle from the house
and sell the bike."

I wouldn't argue with him, since I knew when he mentioned to me the conditions for purchasing the motorcycle he was committed to keeping his promise. Maybe that was just to compromise and keep some peace with my mother, considering she begged him not to buy me the motorbike.

But there always had been one major thing I didn't love about my father that I couldn't forgive him for growing up. It didn't matter that he gave me everything I wanted but my mother didn't. I deeply resented him growing up because he was married to another woman, let alone a German. He also often wouldn't keep his promises and I would be heartbroken. I'd never did get over that easily. Sometimes I'd be suffering for days or even weeks.

I used to wait for him by the front window when he was coming to pick me up. So often, he was either very late or didn't show up at all. I cried hysterically when he didn't come, filled with disappointment and wondering why someone I so admired didn't care about me at all. The rage and frustration threatened to take over me, but my mother would calm me down – saying she would call him and tell him how upset I was.

> "Mom, where is Dad? Why hasn't he come? He was supposed to be here at 4:00 and it's now 5:00. He promised to take me out, buy me a new race car set and take me out to Black Angus, my favorite steakhouse, for dinner. Where is he?"

> "How come he's always really late to pick me up or sometimes doesn't come? He's with his Shiksa isn't he? He never cared about us, only the Deichke. You were always right. He spends all his money and time when he isn't working with her. What type of a father is he?"

She replied by saying:

> "I know you feel really hurt, my shana yingele (beautiful child in Yiddish). Your father is your father, but I'm certain he loves you. He may have had to work, but I know he'll come tomorrow."

> "I will call him and mention he has to come over and take you out. I'll be sure to also tell him how much it hurts you when he doesn't pick you up like he promises. I won't let him forget what he does to you, how he selfishly disappoints you."

That made me feel better for a while, when she confronted my father knowing how much I was hurt, but the pain never stopped. I was a child waiting for my dad, being deeply impatient waiting for him to come over. It destroyed me when he didn't keep his promises.

My mother's bitter hatred didn't only exist for Kathy, but all Germans. I had a friend growing up named Marty Schroeder, who lived near my house. My mother, brother and I took a road trip with his parents – Karl and Lina – and Marty and his sister, Ella. We were driving two cars to California. I was maybe 9 or 10.

As we were riding in the carnear Cheyenne Wyoming, my mother all of a sudden clapped her hand to her ear, in pain and near tears. She moaned, hunching forward against the fabric of her seat in the car. "Momenyu crain, how painful." (Momenyu crain – "I can't take it" in Yiddish). The pain was very intense, almost impossible to bear, and she wanted to go home. But Karl especially wanted us to continue to drive to California.

There was a very bitter argument between my mother and him when we left the hotel we stayed at in Cheyenne. Voices were raised and shouting reverberated within the inside of a gas station we stopped at briefly. Tempers had risen to the point that everyone else in our families and even those around us were getting uncomfortable and maybe afraid of what was happening. I stayed silent, trying not to be noticed, drenched in fear I would be yelled at by one of them. I didn't know what was coming next, but I knew it wouldn't be good.

> "Karl I can't drive anymore, I'm sick, and we have to close all the windows in our car when we're driving. Otherwise, the draft from the air will make my ear infection even worse. We have to go home."

He replied by saying:

> "Rose, I am not going home, I don't have much vacation and we're going to California with or without you. I really don't care. You don't look that sick to me. Do what you want to do."

My mother replied and said:

> "How can you say that, I'm very sick, with a bad cold, I can't hear and we have to drive with the windows closed in our car, traveling in the summer, with no air conditioning. If not, I would probably have to go to the hospital due to my ear infection."

> "Don't you have feelings for people? I know you and your wife's family were Nazis. They probably killed my parents and the rest of my family, not to mention what they did to me. I'll never let Bobby play with your kids anymore. You're a Nazi and you and your family are dead to me."

I don't know whether Karl replied, but my mother no longer would let me play with his kids. That really bothered me so much, since I had played with them almost every day. But I could only listen to what my mother said, since I was a child and not strong enough inside. I had grown up far too dependent on her.

His kids did nothing wrong, but my mother continued to do what she had done, infiltrating us with the deception of her perceptions for Germans – the innocent held accountable for the actions of the guilty. How wrong that was, but that's what she did. Germans who weren't responsible for the atrocities of the Holocaust still were in her eyes. I listened to my mother and stopped playing with Karl's kids. Her trauma really had become my trauma.

Whenever I saw them in the neighborhood after we returned from the car trip, I fixated upon their blond hair, blue eyes and Marty's lederhosen (German leather shorts and suspenders). Their light complexion, Martin's outfit and the trauma from my mother caused my own horror. When I saw them, I thought of German youth believing in the ideology of the Nazi party. I should have missed playing with them – but my mother had convinced me that they stood for the cruelty that had been done to her and her family. I had to protect my mother and our history, but I couldn't realize what it cost.

That should have been the first time I thought of my false reality, no longer able to play with Karl's children, but not for anything they did wrong. I hated Germans, but I had no idea what Oskar Schindler, a German Nazi had done for my mother and so many other Jewish people.

Schindler was not willing to be complicit or concede to the dehumanization of European Jews and the cult-like idealism that fueled deeply conspired Nazi propaganda not only in Europe, but many parts of the rest of the world. Jews were considered to be a disease, a sickness to be eliminated, an inferior race of people who set out to weaken other races and take over the world. Jewish people had no place in Nazi Germany and within most of Europe. Nazi occupation increased nearly everywhere throughout the continent due to the Holocaust.

I don't know what my brother felt during that argument between my mother and Karl, except that he was already living my mother's reality. He was ten years older than me, soft-spoken and kind. I also remember him being timid and terrified of upsetting my mother when he was younger, just as I was.

It often just seemed like it was only the two of us, isolated and facing the world. I could only imagine that he was far more impacted by the hatred my mother inflicted within us for all Germans. He was not as young as I was and the trauma we inherited had been able to penetrate him much more than me. He saw my mother's racist perceptions of Germans as normal behavior – much like I had, but not as deeply as him. There really was no turning back for him anymore, being that much older than I was.

In my brother's final year of college, he suffered a nervous breakdown and was diagnosed with schizophrenia. When I became a little older – being only 13 during the onset of his mental illness, I was certain one of the main causes was all the hatred my brother had for Kathy that was left in him by my mother since childhood. It was probably also due to Harry living in my parent's marriage for 10 years, and how much each of them suffered. But he was still the real collateral damage.

I just didn't understand how she could have done this to him. It was hard to conceive that it was far more intense for him than for me. I don't believe my mother even realized what she did to him. Honestly, how could she knowing the scale of trauma due to her past?

The bitterness I felt towards my stepmother was probably never more unforgettable after one time I was left home alone all day by my mother. It was a month before I turned 13. She left home by 8:30 one Saturday morning in early March and never told me when she left or called all day. I finally phoned my father by 7:30 that night and cried hysterically, telling him he had to come to our house.

> "Mom has not been home all day. I don't know where she is. I have to call the police. You have to come here now. I can't be home alone."

My father replied by saying:

> "I can't come now. I have plans for dinner. She'll be home shortly. I know she'll be home very soon. You can't be a little kid all your life. You have to take care of yourself."

"You have to come here now. I don't know what I will do if you don't come now. Get in your car and come now," I said.

"Ok, I will be there in 20 minutes," he finally relented.

I could hear how reluctant he was to come over to the house and do anything, despite my being panicked and hearing me frantically crying, not knowing where my brother and mother were all day. I was scared, angry and disappointed. Here he was not showing up for me again, letting me down when I needed him. He could really be a very selfish father when I was growing up. If it was on his own time and he wasn't supposed to be visiting me or my brother, he didn't want to be with his kids.

My father's time was pretty limited for his kids, and when he wasn't working he'd spend most of his time with his Shiksa. How much worse could it be than spending time with the person I saw as part of a family who were Nazis? That was the betrayal I felt from him as a father.

In his defense, all the hatred my mother left in me since childhood for my father and Kathy (reciprocated in his feelings towards my mother), I was certain had been a factor in having distance from his kids. As I grew older, I felt that's why he didn't want to be around me and my brother too often. How could he not realize that my mother inflicted her hatred for him in us, done through manipulation?

I came out to my father's luxury, dark brick red car – a newer Riviera – when he got to the house. My stepmother was with him, and my dad knew how upset I would be if she came into our house. They were both dressed for dinner, which I could see despite his car's tinted windows. He wore a gray leisure suit, shirt buttoned up to the very top. Kathy sat next to him wearing a soft yellow dress, her hair done up and deep blue eyes even more accentuated with darker-colored makeup. She was a smart woman and must have known how much my mother blamed her for her past.

But in that moment, I was filled with uncontrollable rage and panic. I was dealing with such pain and abandonment and my father was going out for dinner with his Shiksa. I looked over at him and began to cry hysterically. My eyes were initially fixated on Kathy's blond hair and blue eyes, thinking of her through my mother's lens. I then looked back over at my dad.

> "How could you bring her here? I don't know where my mother is. You're going to leave me alone, go out for dinner with her and you don't care. Where is my mother?"

> "I can't be without her. You left us for that German Shiksa, how could you? You know what mom went through in the Holocaust."

"She lost her entire family to the Nazis and you're with a Shiksa enjoying yourself tonight and I'm deeply suffering. Don't you care about anyone else except yourself?"

My father replied by saying:

"I'm leaving now, Bobby, if you don't calm down. Your mother will be okay. She and Harry will be home soon. You can take care of yourself for a little while longer. If anything else happens, just call my house and leave a message."

After my dad finished speaking, I heard a door open in the back of our house. I had to believe my mother was home, but I didn't know what I would do if she wasn't. I wasn't certain if my brother was also home.

"Mom, Mom is that you? Mom, please, is that you? Are you here? You have to be home."

She responded by saying:

"Yes, Bobby, I'm home and sitting in the kitchen. I am sorry I wasn't home all day, but something happened."

I was still crying when my mother answered, but relieved knowing I was safe now. Growing up, I couldn't be without her. I really panicked when she wasn't around and didn't know where she was. It was a deep seeded fear, one that infested every part of me when that happened, to the point that I couldn't focus on anything else.

She raised me to be as needy as possible for her, and I felt deep anxiety, a pulsating heartbeat in my chest when I was away from her. I knew that was for a reason later in life – she was left without her family as a young teenager in the Holocaust and faced the insecurity of not having anyone. She felt that if she smothered me with affection, I would never leave her. It shouldn't be hard to believe, when you consider that she was living with the trauma of her past, let alone the heartbreaking way her marriage ended.

My dad left when I heard my mother. He turned his back to me and walked to the car without a second glance, and didn't say a single word, his face hard as stone, his suit jacket almost disappearing against the edges of the car. I always felt that his German wife was much more important to him than his kids really ever were. My brother and I were never the priority, and that stung, as much as I tried to hide the tears swelling up in my eyes. His selfishness was very apparent, with him never being around for the hard stuff we faced growing up.

I finally learned from my mother in the next couple days that I was left home alone that day because she was in the hospital with my brother – he had jumped off a building late that Saturday morning due to hearing voices and broke both his knees. It was his first suicide attempt.

When she first told me about it, I felt my stomach drop and the world tilted to the side as I tried to make sense of it. This was my brother – he helped raise me growing up, I looked up to Harry and loved him more than I ever realized, He was well built, like my father and nearly as tall as him, with dark brown hair and a warm smile. My brother was always the first to come to my defense when my mother was about to be lost in a fit of temper over something I'd done wrong. But being told he was sick due to hearing voices? Even then, there was a pit of dread in my stomach. I didn't even know what that meant, except that he was crazy.

My big brother was like a father to me growing up, considering my father wasn't around most of the time. However, the role he played in my life began to vanish later that day, and I feared this probably would severely impact me in the future.

What I learned had happened to him fiercely increased my hatred of my stepmother, and it roiled like a pot of rage inside me, making me so angry I couldn't focus on anything except my anger. It consumed me and was often all I could think about. My father had brought her with him to my house, even as we began to face a crisis with my brother. He must have thought it wouldn't matter to me, that maybe she was someone I could confide in, ask for compassion, or even talk to. I only knew her as someone who wanted to hurt my mother and our family – she was a bitter enemy.

It wasn't until years later that I learned how much I despised Kathy was based upon nothing that was real.

Her family had not been complicit with the Nazis atrocities, what I grew up learning was nothing but the systematic genocide of European Jews. It could not have been a deeper injustice of my mother's vengeance towards her. But the false reality was reality for my mother, while my brother and I were collateral damage for her world.

We were victims and there was nothing anyone could do about it – the two of us were taken captive by our mother, left without the freedom to think differently. We were too young to question what she told us – not having any facts to let us see things differently. Her mistaken reality was forced onto her children and cost us both deeply, though what happened to my brother couldn't be measured.

Ironically, she was doing the same thing that the perpetrators of the Holocaust did to Jews, manifesting their false perceptions of who and what they were. Could I ever forgive her for never sharing the story of her life as a Schindler survivor with us – a Nazi who saved so many Jewish lives rather than murdering them?

When I was 19, I finally learned the truth of my stepmother's life growing up, that I needed to know when I was a child. She was born in Berlin in 1937 and a young child during the Holocaust. Kathy's father was never a Nazi Party loyalist. She describes him as a strong, stubborn man with a trusting smile, who was easy to laughter and would spend weekends taking his children out into the streets to play. He couldn't stand what was happening in Germany – and he lived with deep conviction to his beliefs no matter what, a trait he passed on to his family. Despite living under a fascist government and Nazi ideololgy that had penetrated throughout every part of Germany, he wasn't afraid to share his feelings in public.

One day, two members of the Nazi Army – Wehrmacht came to Kathy's house and knocked on the door. She was maybe 6 or 7, and just finished eating dinner with the rest of her family. They stood in the hallway except her father, who answered the door, and she remembered how afraid the rest of the family had been knowing that two Nazis were standing next to their door. They saluted her father, "Heil Hitler." But he refused to salute them back.

In seconds, both of them grabbed him by his shirt, dragged him into the street, sat him in a chair and shot him in the back of the head. The Nazi who shot him was only standing five to six feet away. Kathy's father died in minutes. Her family couldn't do anything due to fear for their own lives, while they watched in shock what happened outside their living room window. My stepmother was never really able to move past what she'd seen. Whenever she talked about it, she got a distant and unforgettably heatrbreaking look in her eyes.

I had the right to know why I never heard the story of her father growing up. But how could I? Kathy couldn't get within miles of me and my father. He was also too busy taking sides against my mother during their bitter divorce to bother changing what I knew about her. As I've told, my mother had every bit of control over my perceptions of Kathy. It began long before I had any facts to the contrary.

I wished that my mother could have found the help that she desperately needed. But no one discussed or maybe even really knew what trauma was when I was growing up in the 1960's and 70's, let alone what she lived through in the Holocaust. Maybe she would have never done what I blamed her for, especially what she did to my brother – the hatred she left far too deep inside of him, pivotal to his nervous breakdown. Still, I'm not certain therapy would have even helped that much, eventually realizing her losses and what she went through were far too traumatizing for her perceptions to probably ever change. But I also have to say what if it did? How different everything could have been.

But growing up, I couldn't understand how much she was drowning within her past and the reach of personal suffering she grew up with during the Holocaust. The depth of losses were never more unconsionable than in how her life was transformed as a kid.

My mother was 15, living a teenager's life in a deeply loving family, and was forced to face a horror no one would ever really conceive. Two members of the Nazi military knocked on her family's door in January 1941(three years after Kristallnacht) and began yelling "Roust!!!" (German word for "leave"). When my mother would tell the story, I would see a certain look on her face. It was deeply bitter, hollow and made her beautiful face look like it was staring back at something far away.

The Nazis started throwing all of her family's belongings out of their living room window and pushed her father up against a wall, while the rest of the family huddled in the corner, fear shaking inside them to their very cores. My mother, her parents, four sisters and a brother were taken from their home to the Krakow Ghetto on trucks, never to return. She never saw her family again after she was transferred from the Krakow Ghetto to the Plaszow concentration camp in June, 1942. They had been murdered in Belzec and Auschwitz; transported on cattle cars to their deaths in the gas chambers of these extermination camps.

Plaszow was run for a year by the Nazi SS commander Amon Goeth ("Goeth" – "The Butcher of Plaszow") in early 1943. He would often kill people in the prisoner's roll call each morning for no reason. Once he even shot and killed a 10-year-old Jewish boy walking on the grounds of the camp from the balcony of his home. Goeth felt the boy didn't clean one of the bathroom sinks in his home to his satisfaction and shot him in the head after he left.

My mother survived the Plaszow concentration camp and the Holocaust due to Oskar Schindler, because he took certain forced laborers in the prison camp to his enamelware factory in Plaszow ("Emalia"). His factory was a subcamp of the concentration camp. She was considered a skilled worker due to her Blauschein ("blue card"), given to certain Jews in the ghettos that were considered essential workers for the Nazi war effort. The blue cards were given to Jews not always because of their skills, but due to connections which enabled them to get the worker card.

They were temporarily spared, including my mother from being deported out of the Krakow ghetto to the concentration and extermination camps in Poland, including when the ghetto was being liquidated. But when my mother was transported to the Plaszow, Goeth agreed for some of the essential workers in his camp, including her to be transferred to Schindler's new Emalia factory.

I don't know exactly how my mother obtained a Blauschein. I doubt whether she had any specialized skills, since she was 16 in the Krakow Ghetto. Her blue card I believe came through a friend she met in the segregated Jewish quarter, who must have had connections, since she was left at that time without most of her family. My mother was a metal assembly worker for gun production to support the Nazi war effort. She was #139 of the 300 women for the list compiled of the 1248 Jewish lives Oskar Schindler saved. She was a metal assembly worker in Schindler's factory.

Schindler overcame his loyalty to the Nazi Party due to the atrocities he had seen in the Krakow Ghetto and the Plaszow concentration camp run by Goeth. "There was plenty of public evidence of pure sadism with the Nazis behaving like pure pigs," Schindler once said.

My mother probably could had forgiven the German people if she would have overcome some of her trauma and remembered that her life was saved by Schindler – a Nazi. However, the reconciliation she may have found had to be lost when my father left her for Kathy. It was nearly 20 years after the Holocaust. In that moment, her hatred of Germans potentially became much deeper than at any point within her past. She was lost to reason, her past again taking over the present. My dilemma is how much I blamed her, and maybe I didn't have the right to due to her past. All I know is that my brother and I suffered gravely for something she couldn't forget or couldn't see that was in front of her – holding the innocent accountable for the actions of the guilty.

It's funny, my mother always had told me that in the Jewish Bible, one of the guiding principles is that we must never hate. Jewish people are supposed to treat people the same as themselves, a lesson she would teach us often, as we sat together at dinner, talking about the things that should matter to us most. Yet my mother, brother and I deeply hated my stepmother, and every other German. We could never treat them like we'd want ourselves to be treated.

My brother and I were raised by my mother as Orthodox Jews because that was how my mother was raised by her family prior to the Holocaust. The Orthodox strictly observe the Torah. Despite my mother always telling us to live according to two fundamental principles of the Jewish Bible, We Must Never Hate" and "Live With Forgiveness," it couldn't change how she felt towards Kathy and every other German.

I wish she could have realized what her bitter hatred for Kathy, but even more all Germans was really doing to me growing up, let alone my brother. For example, I had trauma for certain colors such as reed green, since it was one of the colors of the Nazis' uniforms. Even the slightest glimpse of the color would send me into a panic and my heart would start racing. I was unable to focus on anything else, becoming utterly consumed with fear, indignation and disgust towards whoever was wearing green. They were my mother's and her family's enemies and now mine.

I also often looked at the color white as a reminder of swastikas. When I heard someone who spoke German or had a German accent, or at times even saw somebody take a large step forward, it would remind me of a Nazi army officer marching.

These were triggers for my nightmares that often woke me in the middle of the night. I'd cry hysterically in my bed as a child and stare out the window for hours, wondering what I could possibly do to protect myself and save the people around me.

Growing up, I used to watch the sitcom Hogans Heroes, which was the story of prisoners in one of the Nazis' prisons, "Stalock 13", during the Holocaust. When I watched the TV program, despite it being a comedy, the Nazi prison guards and their green uniforms triggered many nightmares, which further painted the dehumanizing images of my mother's concentration camp stories.

I was left wondering if there would ever be anything that could change. How would I find forgiveness for how my mother raised me and my brother with unthinkable hatred? The cost was a price that we couldn't afford, even if one day we could both see my stepmother and every other German differently. Would there ever be a point where I knew what the story of *"Schindler's List"* left me with – "That what brings us together can overcome what pulls us apart"? But with that much hatred we grew up with as children, how could anything really change?

CHAPTER II

Awakening – My Perceptions of Change

A brisk spring day in early April 1980 felt like a real turning point for me. When I was 18, the perceptions I had of my mother began to change – though not really enough. I took up jogging since I wanted to lose weight and halfway through the mile - run, the discipline of exercise somehow began to fuel an independence that would start to change my views after all the years of my mother's hatred for Kathy. I physically exerted myself like I never had before. I felt such a runner's high when I was done, which included a two-block sprint at the end of the mile I ran. I was gasping for breath and my body couldn't take it any more, but I finished running with the distance and physical demand I wanted to fulfill.

Growing up, I always considered myself very lazy both physically and mentally. I never exercised much, didn't study hard and worked part-time for my father delivering cars for his auto delivery business – dropping cars off from one used car lot or car dealership to another. It was just a mindless, cush job. I blamed my mother for how I perceived myself as being incredibly lethargic. She never encouraged me to study, work hard, or aspire to my own independence. I really didn't have to think with my own mind. I had been raised to be that dependent upon my mother so that I would never leave her. I felt later in life it was in exchange for accepting all of her feelings of hatred for my father and Kathy. She wanted them to also be mine.

When I finished my run and came in the house I felt awakened when I saw my mother. It had given me a certain detachment from her that I'd never known. The running was something that I'd done – self-fulfillment I'd never felt. Maybe it was a fresh start and a step toward finally having my own lens for the feelings towards my father and Kathy.

That day, the onset of growth I felt after running had given me the independence I'd never known. Somehow it let me feel I finally could take care of myself. I never had any self-confidence growing up. Maybe it was due to being picked on by other kids for being fat when I was younger, my mother's overprotection, or unhealthy affection. I've said what she did was also manipulative – only to see my father and Kathy through her eyes.

My dad called me when I returned home after running, maybe by 8:30 PM. For the first time, I asked how my stepmother was doing. The shock in my father's voice was clear for me asking anything about her. I then found myself hoping they would both come to my high school graduation.

> "I was hoping Kathy might want to join you for my high school graduation. I have seats for both of you."

He replied by saying:

> "What about your mother? She will never let me bring her to the ceremony. It will turn into a tragedy. You know her by now."

> "Well, your seats are in different sections and maybe I can see you separately. That way she won't know you both came." I replied.

I knew the path for change in myself was uncertain but convinced one had begun. Exercise of all things had uncovered a new direction that I hadn't experienced. It was discipline that was changing me. When I was in high school, I would come home from school and the rest of my day consisted of working for my father, that I'd said didn't take much effort, lying around in bed watching TV, doing a little homework and going out with my friends. I was also really fat growing up, but too lazy to do anything about it, even being bullied by other kids in grade school and high school.

Running made me care about my appearance, while my mother didn't care much about hers. But Kathy believed how you looked defined who you were. She was a very attractive 5'6" blond-haired woman, dressed to kill, with rare elegance. My mother was a brunette, with an attractive face, who became pretty heavy when I was an older kid. She was also quite short – 4'11" – and wore old fashioned clothes. Her appearance didn't matter to her, especially a few years after my father left her. I'm also not certain if it ever really did that much her whole life. She grew up in a very traditional Jewish family; her parents were so old fashioned, and by 16 she was living in a concentration camp.

My physical appearance also had been a deep barrier to my friendships when I could no longer stand hanging out with my best friend, Larry, in high school. We would go roller skating at the Axler Roller Rink in Des Plaines. I would generally have to drive, since he didn't have his own car yet. I felt invisible with him one night at the skating rink. There were two women fighting over him that night. When he introduced one of them to me, she only asked if I knew which one of them he thought was more attractive.

Larry was a tall, well-built, very attractive guy, who women would do anything to get close to. But I felt like an embarrassment, especially around him never dating anyone. I believed girls thought I was repulsive. I was 165 pounds, much too heavy for my shorter size – 5'3" – and never dressed well. It was how my mother raised me.

My exercise regimen heavily increased in the spring and summer months prior to leaving for college, often with inhumane intensity. I felt the exercise was mandated to maintain the growth I began to feel back in early April. I had to push myself harder, feeling it would give me continued detachment from my mother and acceptance with my friends. The physical discipline also began to change a little of the deep bitterness that I held for my stepmother. The strong value I began to apply to physical appearance and her commitment to that value turned into a model for growth, which started to define me.

The intense workout each day consisted of a three-mile run, with a two-block sprint at the end of my jog, then sit-ups and push-ups until my hands and torso were bleeding. I would also repeat the sit-ups and push-ups late at night – nearly as many as my mid-day workout - and sometimes run a few more miles before I went to bed. My daily diet was a few bananas, a yogurt and a diet Coke or two. I lost 37 pounds in 6 weeks. When my dad saw me once after I lost the weight, he told me, "You have to be on drugs."

There were times that I felt if I didn't do this tormenting physical routine every day, I wouldn't feel right, like I didn't exist – I couldn't live with myself. As I've told, the self-discipline was fulfillment that I never had. I convinced myself If I didn't exercise that obsessively, or worse, rested for a day, I would regress into someone I couldn't live with – an unmotivated, lazy, co-dependent, fat kid, like I felt growing up.

The months prior to high school graduation built upon my changing perceptions of my father, but primarily my stepmother. I had finally taken a few steps to get to know her, apart from my mother's baseless world of darkness which affected how I'd seen her. I asked my dad more about her, where she was born, a little about her family and that I might not mind visiting him when he was home and she was there.

The first time I visited my father at his home and Kathy was there, our conversation was pretty short. But I did tell her after I talked to her for a little while, that she didn't seem like the person my mother told me she was. There wasn't much a response from her except telling me, "your mother is your mother and I can't help that." After what she said, I wished that I would have heard her say something different. I would have felt much better. But how could I expect her feelings towards my mother for that long would just go away.

When I came home and told my mother I saw my father and Kathy I panicked. I became fixated on the deep rage clearly seen across her face after I told her. But somehow, I regained my composure and said that I wanted to see both of them, if she was there when I'd go to my father's. I knew my mother was beside herself, but I just didn't care anymore. After so many years of seeing them through her eyes, maybe now I realized that never was who they really were.

> "You saw your father in his home this afternoon and the Deichke was home. You told me that you would never have anything to do with her.

> "Your father left me for someone whose family probably helped murder mine, not to mention what they did to me. Yet you go to visit him, when she's home with him. You can't go see him when he's with his Shiksa."

> I replied:

> "Mom, I understand what happened to you, but when I talked to her, she was not mean. She's his wife. I know how much you lost and what you've suffered, but I can no longer not visit him when she's home. I just can't. If you loved me, you'd begin to understand."

She didn't say much after what I told her. Maybe she knew that I was changing and felt if she manipulated me with guilt and betrayal for seeing them together – like she'd always pretty easily done – I'd finally realize what that had done to me. How could I forgive her?

But I wasn't ready to accept Kathy due to how I was raised. Still I began to feel that I wasn't seeing her anymore exactly the same way my mother felt about her. I also knew that by spending only a little time with my father – when we went out for lunch, dinner, or a ballgame – I'd never really come to know him. I had to visit him when he was home, not only at his office. It didn't matter whether or not my stepmother was there. If I saw him more often when they were together, maybe I would get to know Kathy differently than how I was raised.

My views began to change slowly, and it was a long process. It all came back to my mother, and how she convinced me that if how I felt ever changed, she wouldn't there for me. I wasn't certain how that would materialize, but I didn't want to find out. The insecurity she left me with would have me panic and question how I could live without her. How would I be taken care of? How would I have a place to eat or sleep? The first glimpse of when your life in front of you begins to turn is both terrifying and exhilarating.

For most people, graduation day is filled with celebration and gratitude for the accomplishment of finishing a four-year chapter in your life – how you've grown and what you've become in preparation for the next stage in life. I was proud of those achievements, while also feeling deeply torn since my mother and brother were in one section of the audience and my father and stepmother were seated in another. I always knew our family was not normal; my parents were not only divorced but they couldn't stand each other, and there was the depth of my mother's trauma due to the Holocaust.

But they shouldn't have left me in such a compromised position. I desperately wished they could have put aside their differences, even for a couple of hours, to recognize the achievement of the son they had together. But a tortured marriage and even more vengeance towards each other after they were divorced couldn't change their feelings. While I wished they could have sat together, that would have been an unforgettable tragedy. My mother didn't even know I invited my dad and Kathy to the graduation. I couldn't tell her – knowing how I grew up, she would have seen that as heartbreaking betrayal.

My high school graduation was in Niles West High School's 15,000-seat football stadium covering an acre of land. The premises were very spread out, which I considered a blessing for each of my parents not having to see each other, or worse, interact. I couldn't be more relieved knowing they were seated on opposite sides of the stadium.

I was very preoccupied with where my father and stepmother were in the audience. I hoped my father and even to some extent Kathy were proud of my four years of educational achievement, and that I was going to college. As I began to feel a little differently towards my father and especially Kathy, what my mother thought just mattered a little less than it did growing up.

I began to care about their opinions, despite the fact that they'd never particularly mattered the way I was raised. I was getting to know people that I had never really known. Until I was 18, I had never got anywhere near Kathy. I didn't know what my mother would have done to me if I had. I didn't see my father that much outside of a few days at work and going out for a good time. He never asked me very much about school. But I finally began to care about what he thought of me and shockingly my stepmother a little. Still I knew that might not last.

My mother's imprint of manipulation that she left inside me was that deep, even if I began to care more about what my father and a little what Kathy thought of me. But to really see them differently, I'd have to overcome my mother's trauma that had penetrated every bit of me – manifested in hatred, that began when I was a child. You can be shaped for the rest of your life by what you learn when you're that young from a parent. I didn't know what else to believe, or know any better, except what my mother told me.

The next few months before I left for college I just continued to grow farther apart from my mother. I worked for my father in the summer, came home, worked out almost until I couldn't and then went out with my friends. After growing up that dependent on my mother, I barely mentioned a word to her when I was home. I couldn't have been happier, feeling the exercise and maybe getting a little older had continued to give me confidence that I'd be able to stand on my own. I couldn't wait to leave home.

The day I packed and left for college, I didn't even feel like I'd miss my mother. That brisk day in April before I graduated finally enabled me to begin to find a little independence, perspective and detachment from my mother's deep influences. However, I lost some of that before I left. It's when she promised to send me a $225 allowance for spending money every two weeks in my first semester.

I thought it was plenty of money to be giving me, while being away at school. I wouldn't have any expenses, except for laundry and going out with my friends. It was her way for me to feel secure being away from home for the first time. But as I grew older, I felt it was also another form of manipulation to let me know how much I needed her. It left me with guilt for leaving her. Given how she raised me to feel I couldn't be without her, she knew I would feel guilty. Whatever growth I'd found in feeling that I no longer needed to depend on her, apparently was more fragile than I realized.

I was that afraid the money might impact some of the growth in me before I left for college. You would expect a mother to want to teach her son how to stand on his own when he leaves home for the first time. Instead, I would come to realize the financial security wasn't to help me and detach from my mother in the way I needed. I can't say enough how much she wanted me to know that I still couldn't manage without her. As I became older, I felt certain that the money was also a bribe to not turn against her and leave home permanently. She was pretty afraid that when I left I'd begin to have a relationship with Kathy, even after I'd only seen her once. She felt that Kathy hated her as much as my mother hated my stepmother. That probably triggered her real fear. I'd get to know Kathy and turn against her.

I arrived at college – Jacksonville University in Florida during early September for my first semester. It was a humid, near sauna-like 95-degree day and not typical for weather back in Chicago. The campus wasn't that large – maybe four or five miles, being a smaller private university. It was a pivotal day for me: I had left home for the first time – nearly 2,200 miles away from my mother. I thought of how far away I was from her that day, when I arrived at the campus.

The deep memories of how dependent on her I was growing up came to mind. All those years, how I couldn't be without her, needing that affection and protection – never wanting to know the nightmare of living without her. But I've told that I had grown a little in my senior year of high school, finding some detachment from my mother. I wasn't letting her control me as much as she did. I began to see the way she felt about Kathy maybe had never been deserved.

College was a new environment and during the first couple months I found myself partying nearly all my waking hours when I wasn't studying. I had also partied a little bit in high school – smoking pot and drinking with my friends on the weekends. But while being away from home, I really took advantage of the freedom.

A few days a week before lunch and my gut-wrenching workouts in the mid-afternoon of the Jacksonville humidity, I'd smoke a little bit of pot with Roberto. He was one of my dorm friends. I had still continued to workout that obsessively after my senior year of high school.

Smoking a little pot helped take the edge off a bit – but not too much though, before the workouts. After my friends in the dorm and I studied at the library every weeknight, we'd also meet for a few drinks at the Rathskeller – a college campus bar. On the weekends, I'd generally get drunk and a little stoned at frat parties. I was a non-conformist, particularly when I thought of frats – similar to my friends - but I just wanted to go to their parties, despite that I never considered joining one.

My roommate Bill was nearly idolized by my dorm friends. He carried himself as a role model, telling everyone he was a straight-A student, a star baseball player in high school – heavily recruited by colleges - and all women loved him. Cam, Roberto, Jim and Percey were my other really good friends. They and Bill were my newly replaced family, being away from home.

Roberto was 5'9", medium build, with very short blond hair – nearly a crew cut – a good athlete, who studied and partied hard. He was Puerto Rican, spoke Spanish and lived with an affinity for his cultural background. He always told me about growing up in a Puerto Rican neighborhood of Miami. He got into a few fights that he instigated with a few Latinos who weren't Puerto Rican where he lived growing up. They were talking smack about his culture and he didn't even reply. Nearly reflexively, he just started pushing and hitting them to defend his heritage.

I hung out with him a lot and also looked forward to smoking (a few bongs) with him at night after classes. He was opinionated even about me and I soon learned that not having grown up wealthy, he was envious of people that had. He always made fun of my clothes, that were old fashioned. He said if I continued to wear flood plants and shirts that were baggy, I'd never pick up girls.

Cam was 6 feet, slender build – no body fat and a very good looking guy. He was soft-spoken, a drummer and as you'd expect, didn't have to say much to pick up girls. His family was very rich; he grew up in Wilmette and was the only one of my friends with a car, and close to brand new.

Roberto and Cam were roommates, and I knew Roberto was a little jealous of him due to his looks and money. He was a better student than Cam, studying harder and just understanding things better, but that didn't really matter to Roberto. Cam's wealth and looks made Roberto see him as a "pretty boy" and a "trust fund" kid. Those were qualities he valued but deeply resented on the surface.

The memories I had of feeling too dependent on my mother when I first came to college had disappeared. Any thought of returning home never entered my mind. I couldn't have been happier being away at school, with new friends and feeling that I was continuing on a path of growth. There was real freedom, being away from home. It wasn't only living on my own; it was more the confidence that I no longer needed my mother. I felt that I'd finally separated from all her years of overbearing affection and false security that made me feel like I couldn't survive on my own. I had become independent, but in some ways probably not. I was living in a dorm-room apartment with a roommate and wasn't paying for rent, food or tuition.

During the next few months, I soon discovered that Bill's prestigious accomplishments were too iconic to be real. They were very cleverly contoured, deeply exaggerated realities. He was a really clever, charming fraud.

My college dorm friends, despite feeling like my surrogate family – being away from home began to bully me. It was maybe a few weeks into the semester and continued to increase in the next few months. I was getting bullied due to being short – 5'5" – while every one of my buddies was 5'9" to 6'1". My being Jewish also played a heavy role, even with Roberto. That was surprising since he deeply valued his minority heritage, being Puerto Rican. I guess there had to be a double standard. But he was pretty conceded.

The abuse generally took the form of calling me names, such as "tiny," "wimp" and once I heard them refer to me as "Jew Man." There were times after hearing the bullying that I couldn't understand how my "friends" could be that evil. I thought they were my friends, but how could they be? I really didn't know what to do. I didn't think that I was capable of defending myself, remembering when I was bullied in school for being a fat kid, knowing how dependent I was on my mother growing up.

As a prank, Roberto and a new friend, Rich, leaned a two-foot garbage dumpster against my dorm-room door, filled with water and a foot of garbage, and then knocked. I opened the door and the water and garbage from the dumpster spilled all across the floor of my room.

What my friends had done to me also returned to me feeling like when I was a kid in grade school, often hating myself being picked on continually at recess for being really fat. I felt that I was different, not one of the cool kids, being obese while the other kids weren't. It was the first time in college I wished my mother was there to protect me from being harassed. After the bullying and what my friends did, I felt like I almost couldn't manage being there without her. I couldn't stop remembering always being that needy for her. When I was picked on in school, I could run to her, cry and feel protected. But I wish she had taught me how to stand up for myself, which I'd needed to do, especially now.

While I was away at school, I didn't talk much to my mother. I wanted some distance from her. Even when I felt at times how much I needed her - becoming more afraid after the bullying intensified. I talked to my father, but not Kathy. Despite beginning to get to know her a little right before I left for college, she wasn't one of my parents and how could I even accept her? Still, I had continued detaching from some of my mother's perceptions of her. I didn't feel as much like she had stolen my father from me or that her family was directly responsible for what my mother went through in the Holocaust. I no longer felt the hatred for her to the extent of what I had grown up with since I was a little kid. The distance away from my mother had weakened how much she infiltrated my mind with despise for Kathy.

My father and I talked briefly about school and studying – if I liked being away from home and returning for another semester. I mentioned that my grades were very good – carrying a B+ average - but didn't answer his second question, except that I looked forward to returning after Thanksgiving break. I didn't want to mention too him how afraid I was becoming due to the bullying. I wanted him to feel that I was as tough as him, to know I could stand up for myself. There was also no way I would say anything about how much I partied with my friends, since he wouldn't believe my grades were that good.

I told him what he needed to hear, so that he wouldn't force me to come home, especially when he knew my grades were that good. However, the bullying became much worse during the semester and began to hit really hard in late October. I began to feel coming back home was becoming more and more of a better option. I didn't want to continue to live in fear. But I hadn't even considered my growth, that continued in college might be lost when I came home. I just began to feel that I needed my mother's protection.

I had two fist fights with my dorm friends during the second month at school. They were primarily related to their antisemitic harassment. The worst fight was pretty bloody, which began when Bill was drunk one night. His inebriation only inflated an intense dislike for me. I even overheard him talking to one of our friends and saying maliciously that he needed to "beat up the Kike one night."

We were in our 350 square-foot dorm room, and I asked him if I could move some of my clothes by his bed, since I didn't have room in my drawers.

"What the fuck for? You have plenty of room," he said. "No, I don't, my drawers are full. Can't you see?" I said.

He shoved me up against the only window of our tiny dorm, but I shoved him back. Then he tried to wrestle me to the ground, punching me in the head a few times and I punched him harder back. He finally grabbed me hard enough, where, losing my balance in a headlock, he pushed me to the ground. I still kept hitting him while he was on top of me and finally pushed my hands across his face so I could move him off me a little bit. I continued to push his head with some more leverage, and after several punches to the face, I finally pushed him off me. We stood up and looked at each other, each having plenty of cuts with lengthy strands of blood across our faces.

Roberto, who heard us shouting in his dorm room, which was a few doors down across the hall from ours, finally came into our room and put his hands out to distance us from each other. He was standing in the middle to separate us. Despite both of us wanting to continue beating up each other, with Roberto between Bill and I, we eventually calmed down. He made us agree not to start anything up again – finally breaking up the fight.

I stood my ground during our bloody confrontation, despite him being 6'1" and 190 pounds versus me being 5'5" and 130. My deep skin cuts, black and blue marks and sprained hand from our fight hurt for 10 days. The fight with Bill had really caused me to become much more afraid of being around him or any of my other friends in the dorm.

After what happened, I had a constant fear of continued intimidation, violent confrontations and becoming isolated. I also panicked that if there were more fights with Bill, or any of my other friends, I didn't know how I'd be able to continue to hang out with them. Though standing up to him, which I didn't think I could do, made me feel safer.

But my anxiety due to the growing fear of continuing to be abused wouldn't let me realize what the costs might be going home. It got to the point where I just had to come back to where I felt that I was protected.

The excruciating workouts that continued in college were to build upon detachment from my mother and the feelings of inadequacy since childhood. The exercising also intensified due to the bullying. They made me feel a little stronger to not be afraid and stand up for myself when things turned violent.

Near 3:30 PM everyday, I would run on the outdoor track next to my dorm for three miles in the 90-degree heat and humidity of Northern Florida. After running, I lifted weights and finished with three sets of 150 sit-ups on the highest incline of the "abs" bar in a 150-square foot mini-gym. The one-room, dingy gym was in the basement of my dorm and didn't even have air conditioning.

Piles of sweat covered the gym floor, and stained blood covered my torso when I completed the two-hour abusive workout. It began to feel like suffering, while exhilarating (the euphoric "runner's high"), and the exercise remained a ritual in life, if only to neutralize how I felt sometimes about myself and to feel accepted by my college friends. It also increasingly changed my perspective of my stepmother. There was more of me than even before that wanted to measure up to her – knowing how much she valued physical appearance.

My restriction of food also continued in college. I enjoyed a tiny meal for dinner and a piece of fruit near bedtime to hit my daily 800 calories. No lunch or breakfast. I really believed if I was a physical specimen, my dorm friends would see me as one of them. It would relieve my distorted perception of feeling different. I felt that's what I had to for them to stop harassing me. But if nothing else, at least I'd be better able to stand up to them. There were times, even with my insanely restrictive dietary habits and physical regimen, that I couldn't change my deeply held views of being too fat and that I didn't look normal.

I was insecure for not only how I looked, but I also felt my independence in college was still fragile. The $225 allowance every two weeks my mother sent me also made me feel at times as insecure as I was growing up. As I'd said, I felt her generosity was only a means to feel dependent on her that I couldn't live without my mother. Even over 2000 miles away I felt her control.

My mother had well-conceived ways to make sure I wouldn't leave her permanently and financial security was one of them. Her constant fear was that when her kids were old enough to live independently, she'd be alone. There was a part of me that wished I didn't blame her. How could anyone not be that damaged? She was alone at 16; no family and the unconscionable suffering of living her teenage life in the Holocaust. Who wouldn't be that afraid of being alone the rest of their lives?

As I grew older, her manipulation by the overprotection afforded me growing up, sometimes couldn't let me help – as morbid as it sounds, but draw parallels to how the Nazis deeply manipulated Jews during the Holocaust. The Nazis used false realities so that the Jews wouldn't resist the atrocities they would be subject to in the concentration camps. This included telling them they would have a better of way of life if they came to the concentration camps, rather than staying in their own cities being devastated by the war in Europe. Some Jews voluntarily came to the camps, believing what the Nazis told them, not knowing the atrocities and genocide that were occurring.

They would also trick the Jews so that they would remain complacent when they were being led to the gas chambers. The Nazis told them they were going to take a shower and would feel better. It had to be that easy to manipulate the Jews and other prisoners when they arrived in the camps, after being in a cattle car when they were deported that suffocated some of them.

I know the comparison of my mother's manipulation and how the Nazis deceived Jews is not a practical analogy. But with how fragile I grew up and feeling it was done by my mother intentionally, it actually felt later in life that it couldn't be seen much different. I turned to my mother for emotional and financial support and often felt that was exploited, knowing how much I needed her. What she did let me feel secure, but I wasn't.

After the bullying, particularly the fights and being obsessed when something would happen next, I couldn't wait to go home. How much I wished when I came home for Thanksgiving break, that it would have been earlier. The first night home I went out to dinner with my mother and Harry.

From the moment I saw her, I felt protected and loved; there was not even a moment when I remembered my mother's darkness. Her smothering affection and not to have the constant fear of worrying about my college friends let me feel how deeply protected I felt growing up. I couldn't even remember why I was that excited to leave for college in the first place.

In the next couple days, I couldn't get enough of my mother's abundant nurturing, which was only reinforced by her many years of overbearing affection. It was a needed break from the abuse of my supposed friends in the dorms. I became increasingly certain that I wouldn't return to school in Jacksonville next semester and come back home, enrolling in a local college.

The feeling of unrelenting intimidation due to the abuse that had grown violent became far more than I could cope with anymore. I was blind; I couldn't see how the benefits of returning home would potentially come at a regrettable cost. I felt going home was the only real choice I had. I just needed to feel safe, which my mother had always done for me. But if she only would have thought about what was best for me rather than for her – even temporarily putting aside her fears of the past.

I also had become convinced living with my mother was in my best interest and sustainable, even for the three and a half years I had left of college. I didn't know any better; ever since I was little, whenever I was in fear, running for her protection was my only defense. In life, there are decisions where you jump out of the fire and into the inferno, not even knowing you're entering into far more danger than what you've escaped.

I came back from Thanksgiving break to school, but the entire time I couldn't wait to move back home. I only thought about the security again it would give me, but couldn't see what it might cost. I went out a few times with Bill and my other dorm room friends, who were not as abusive the final three weeks before winter break. Maybe they felt I had suffered enough until next semester.

Bill and I to a certain extent reconciled from our fight before I left for break – though perhaps not really. I knew he still viewed me as a wimp, and a kike by what I heard him say to others, even a few times after what happened. I just didn't want to fight anymore and knew I wouldn't be coming back there. The plan to leave in a few weeks meant it wasn't worth the risk, even if he confronted me. I would no longer stand up for myself if he provoked me.

I didn't tell Bill and my other dorm friends I wasn't coming back next semester, because I didn't want to explain to them why I was leaving. I thought they would see me as a coward just running away from them. I was also afraid that if they found out I was leaving, there would be one last violent incident to reinforce their racist perspectives - feeling they were better than me. The exertions of power by them to represent that I was inferior – racial and otherwise.

In December, I came home from school. I went back to work for my father in his auto delivery business and researched local colleges to enroll in for next semester. I finally decided to take a semester off from school and work for my father, since it got to be too late to register for college. It didn't bother me being around my mother more when I came home. Her overbearing affection, after being violently intimidated seemed like I had been rescued. But after coming home, it didn't take long for me to lose how I'd grown in my senior of high school, which continued in college.

My father was probably glad I was back home. He didn't have to continue to pay for out-of-state tuition, and I was no longer in Florida. It's where people often vacation due to the weather, and he worried I wouldn't really focus on college and just party too much. He might have also thought, despite going back home to my mother, I'd grown in beginning to change my perceptions of him – and may be even more importantly of Kathy.

But unknowingly, I was moving backwards, not standing up for myself and running back home for my mother's protection – her deeply, manipulative affection and false sense of security. How was I that blind to not know how much this might affect me – just as I reached a turning point and finally began to see my father and Kathy a little differently than how I'd grown up? How could I also know that what happened even in the next two months would have me wanting to deeply reconsider my decision?

CHAPTER III
Leaving Home Never to Return

I came home after working for my father one day, being an unbearably cold winter afternoon in early January 1981. I went upstairs to my mother's room and talked to her for nearly twenty minutes, when she said one of my friends from high school called. His name was Mike Schuman. She didn't mention to him I wasn't home or would call back. Her conversation with him was much more delusional.

"Is Bob home?" Mike said.

"No, he's not and don't ever call here again. You're part of "The Line", which follows me everywhere like those who I thought were my friends. I know what you're saying to people who are part of them," she replied. Then she hung up on him.

What she was referring to were certain friends of hers, who she believed were Nazi spies had been watching her and planned to let the Gestapo know where she was hiding to be deported to a concentration camp. When she had these conversations with me growing up, I had to find a way to stop listening. I couldn't believe we had these discussions. They were just so crazy. I lost deep respect her for as a parent when I heard these stories – they were like deranged conspiracies.

I questioned her again as to why she hung up the phone after Mike called.

"He is one of them."

"One of what?" I said.

"He's one of the spies, with my friends like Paula and Chaike, who are watching me. They'll tell the Gestapo where I'm hiding."

"They were my friends, but they're spying on me. I couldn't be friends with them any longer. How could they be my friends? They're actually spies for the Nazis. You can't be friends with Mike either. He's one of them."

I just became angrier with every breath I felt, until I ran out of the room. I didn't say a word to her and had to leave the house. After I left, I called my father. I was frantic and became hysterical.

> "My mother is nuts. She believes there are Nazi spies who were her friends and now she thinks my close friend Mike is also one of them. Mike is spying for the Gestapo, she said."

> "She told me he'll let them know where she was hiding. Dad, I can't stay at home any longer."

"You don't have any options, you have to leave now. You're not safe. Where are you going?" My father said.

"To a motel. I also want to rent an apartment, probably in Chicago. It will be easier for working with you and maybe cheaper than living in the suburbs," I said.

My father replied:

> "Okay, when I see you at work tomorrow, we'll discuss what you want to do further. You have my support."

I went some place not far away from where I lived that night. I knew I wasn't going back home. I didn't want any more contact with my mother for the rest of my life. But I couldn't really understand how much my mother was suffering from her Holocaust survivor trauma that was beginning to spiral. I was running for my own life.

It felt like I had finally escaped when I left home. Meanwhile, I didn't know what might lie ahead. Would I continue to take care of myself and be able to leave my mother's delusional behavior? Or would I go back to her manipulative, overbearing affection that falsely protected me growing up, her vengeance for my stepmother and spiraling trauma that also might begin to affect me?

That night I knew I also couldn't go back home, panicking that otherwise my fate would be my brother's. My stomach tightened into thick knots, I felt my heart beating, like it was vibrating uncontrollably, and even unaware for awhile I was heavily sweating. I was just overcame by anxiety: I had to leave now. My brother lived at home for a while, but wasn't consistently stable. In the five years after his nervous breakdown which happened when I was 13, he recovered for awhile but then went back to psychiatric hospitals. After being discharged, he was better for six months but then relapsed and never recovered again.

He came home after working for my father one evening and something happened. It made me pretty certain he wasn't going to stay healthy after he left the last psychiatric hospital. He was 26 and I was 16. His thoughts had become more distraught the past two to three days. After he left home later that night, my mother got a call by 12:00 midnight that he was in the emergency room. He had slit his wrists with a razor and was bleeding deeply.

It was his second and final suicide attempt. Luckily, he didn't kill himself; his cuts were bandaged and he spent a few days in a psychiatric hospital and then was released. But after what he did to himself again, I felt things weren't going to change.

As his fate became more certain, he was no longer mentally there; maybe not surviving his second suicide attempt would have been a better ending. He wouldn't have had to suffer anymore. I also wouldn't have had to see some of what he went through, or my father, who felt the same way. Were we that selfish? But I don't think my mother sometimes what he was going through. How could she, especially now with her own trauma spiraling.

I never could accept what happened to him, especially given his potential. He was a dean's list student in college, had a diligent work ethic, very good looking and how much he loved his brother. But I couldn't regret my decision to leave home, despite what was happening to him, let alone my mother's continued mental decline. I knew what probably lied in store for me if I didn't leave.

When I thought about how she was significantly to blame for his illness, I just seethed with rage – my face looked redder than fire. Harry was the real collateral damage for the intense hatred she inflicted on him that was mentally unsustainable. Something had to finally give and how it did when he was 23 and I was 13.

The next morning after I left home, I rented an apartment in Chicago near the lakefront, maybe two miles away from my home in Lincolnwood. It wasn't really much, but I couldn't have felt better not to be home any longer. That couldn't have meant more to me – feeling that I knew my brother's fate, but I'd rescued myself by leaving. By moving out, I'd also finally escaped my mother's long history of insanity that began to suffocate me. They were delusions that I had lived with since childhood.

My new apartment was tiny, a one-bedroom, 450 square foot space. It was a 22-unit, brick, mixed-use building built in the 1930's My view from the bedroom window looked down over rusted metal garbage cans, garages and parking lots of similar older buildings in the back alley. The front window looked over a main street – Devon Avenue.

The rent for the apartment was $150 / month, and it was not very well maintained, but relatively cheap compared to what anyone would pay for a similar place. It was worth every penny, knowing I wouldn't be going home. That morning, when I signed the lease for the apartment, I called my father and told him I rented a place. I knew he wanted to talk to me first, but I couldn't wait. I wanted to know that I had some place to live after I woke up in the morning and left the motel.

My father congratulated me when I called him.

> "I'm really happy you rented a place. I'll stop by tomorrow night."

I remember later that day waiting for my father, celebrating after purchasing groceries, with an ecstatic smile on my face.

> "I have my own apartment and I'm never going home. I don't have to see my mother ever again and live anymore with her fucked up illness."

I was celebrating, but also panicked, being alone in an apartment within a neighborhood that wasn't nearly as safe as living in the suburbs. Our home in Lincolnwood was in the north suburbs of Chicago. The area was pretty affluent. As I finished jogging a few miles on a snowy winter night in January, feeling such a runner's high, there was a glow in my eyes – even when I looked around my little two-room apartment.

That night, I couldn't have felt more freedom from what my mother had put me through. Her deranged mind and hatred had fed inside me like a parasite. It poisoned some of my feelings towards my father and especially Kathy. But I also panicked due to my own insecurity. I just couldn't slow down the constant doubts that I wouldn't survive on my own, having been so dependent upon my mother growing up.

When I moved out, despite the way I did – in rage and rushing to get the hell out – it also left me feeling really guilty. I was deeply conflicted not having at least some compassion for my mother's endless pain, She had also finally been overcome by her trauma. I questioned how I could not feel that way, after knowing what she endured.

I saw her face that first night in my apartment, watching the tears racing down her face when she'd told me how her parents, sisters and a brother died in Auschwitz and the Belzec death camps. I also had the same image of her, remembering how often she told me and my brother that she didn't know why my father left her for a German woman.

My dad came to my new place by about 6:30 the next night and rang the doorbell for 10 deafening seconds. It sounded like ambulance sirens. Once he entered, he walked briefly into the narrow living room, looking down the front window at the heavy traffic on Devon. He turned and walked into the kitchen and bathroom, which were both very old-fashioned. The cabinets and appliances were more than 20 years old. He then walked to the bedroom and pulled up the one window shade, noticing the back alley and the rusted, cracked garbage cans. Then he looked directly at the clear plastic covering my bedroom as a door and walked back to the living room.

When my father questioned me as to certain details of the apartment, cost, lease, etc., I replied with a calm voice, but panicked waiting for his next sentence. I really thought he'd feel my apartment was a shit hole and tell me to find another place or live with him and Kathy. Instead, he looked over at me with a calm smile on his face.

> "Not that bad for your first place. I want Kathy to visit the apartment. She'll let us know what she thinks and doesn't mind that you live here at least for a year. I know you signed a one-year lease."

I wanted to but didn't ask him how I would break the lease, if Kathy wanted me to leave after she saw my place. I figured since he owned a very successful business, he would understand what had to be done to get out of it.

The second night in my place, I was still so nervous being alone. How could I expect anything different, after all the conditioning by my mother since childhood that wouldn't let me stand on my own? Her feeling of protection was that much of an addiction growing up; I couldn't be without it. But maybe I was finally really growing – no longer a victim of her trauma that smothered me with affection and to feel safe.

In my first semester of college, I lived away from home, but I had a roommate and a good number of friends, at least initially. I never really felt alone when I'd been away. But as I've mentioned, I had become afraid of my dorm friends.

Kathy visited my apartment late Wednesday afternoon. It was maybe 4:30 or 5:00 when she arrived. It was particularly surprising, still having lots of daylight radiating on a winter day in January. She and my father rang my disturbingly noisy buzzer for 10 long seconds. It was identical to how the doorbell sounded and the buzzing lasted when my father came over earlier in the week.

I answered the door with dripping, sweaty palms from uncontrollable nervousness. Kathy's most important values were looks, elegance and a meticulous lifestyle that no one could mirror. Her judgment could be deeply critical. I guess feeling that panicked was reasonable, as I was thinking the worst. I knew that she might feel my place was a disgusting shithole.

She walked into my little two-room apartment with my dad, raised her head, stood in the middle of the living room and then turned to my father. She didn't walk anywhere else in my place – bedroom, kitchen, etc. Her eyes were fused with a vicious glow and there was anger in her face that I'd never seen before, as she looked squarely at my father. I felt she was intimidating him.

> "How could you let him rent this place? It's a dump, no one can live here. If Bobby has a lease, let's tear it up. He can't be here another moment. He has to move, and I'll help him find another apartment."

> "Some places in the suburbs are really nice, modern and no comparison to how much cleaner they are than this filth. Maybe near where we used to live in Des Plaines?"

Kathy then looked at me with disgust and a smirky, condescending smile.

> "Nay, nay (nay meaning "no" in German), oh my God. How did your mother raise you? No taste. I guess you're just like your mother, but maybe I can't blame you."

She laughed at me while telling me what she said – having made fun of me and my mother. I just stood there and didn't know what to say, except that I was pretty dam hurt she said those things.

> "What type of a person can rent an apartment like this? The carpets are deeply stained, the floors are cracked, the bedroom door is a plastic cover and the appliances were built during the early 1900's."

"They're not even as modern as my home in Berlin growing up in the 1930's and 40's. The oven and refrigerator are covered with rust."

"Doesn't he have any sense?" she said to my father and yelled with rage that was nearly physical seen."

He didn't say a word to Kathy. I was disgusted with him that he couldn't defend me, especially after he'd seen my apartment and told me it wasn't bad. But I knew there were times he was pretty scared of her. They fought about things like every couple. But he loved her looks, elegance, taste in most things, how meticulous she was and her being a great cook. I knew he never wanted to lose her.

The next day I went to see some places in Des Plaines with my stepmother and within an hour we found a studio apartment in a relatively new building complex. The apartment was clean and painted, with a fresh coat of floor wax and the floors weren't cracked.

We signed a one-year lease for the studio and then I went with my father to my place in Chicago. He was able to negotiate with the landlord to pay an $80 lease termination fee. I was no longer responsible for the lease. He agreed to pay half the rent for the studio in Des Plaines, which was $350 / month. It was more than twice what I paid for my apartment in the city. I couldn't afford the studio with what I made only working for him. I couldn't have been more grateful that he would pay half the rent, since I knew my place in Chicago was a shit hole that wasn't in a good neighborhood. It was a real adjustment from living in Lincolnwood – being an affluent suburb.

After we left my new place, Kathy told me we'd look for furniture and paintings to decorate my apartment. But I would have to return home for five days, since the lease wouldn't start until next Tuesday. I was so happy renting the place, but terrified my mother wouldn't let me come back home.

It was a dangerous proposition, going home after having left in the evening a few days ago, with uncontrollable rage and not telling my mother where I was going. I didn't know what would happen, knowing that she had so much power over me growing up. I had always lived with her deeply manipulative ways to control some of my mind.

I never asked if I could stay with my father when I left home, since I knew that I needed my independence. Most importantly, my perceptions of Kathy hadn't really changed, despite all she was doing. If I couldn't accept her, how I could live with her?

I came back home Thursday evening being that afraid I wouldn't be able to leave again – trembling and nearly frozen when I walked in the front door. I said nothing to my mother when I came home. I went to my room and she asked me why I left. Then, regaining my composure, without any compassion for her I replied, "I had to leave." She questioned what I meant three or four times. I didn't answer and only would say a few words to her when I decided to leave the house later that night. I wasn't ready for any more questions.

"I have to leave now. I am going to meet one of my friends."

She probably knew by the way I left the house, being next to hysterical and didn't come back home, nothing would change my mind to get me to continue to live with her. How could she feel differently?

It was still best not answering before I left. If I'd talked with her more, I might have believed that leaving her was maybe even unconscionable betrayal, knowing her influences had penetrated that far inside me. As I've told, her manipulation since childhood I felt was a tactic of extortion to prey upon my guilt and insecurity. Apparently, that deep vulnerability had never left me. But I was compromised, beginning to get to know Kathy in a different way than only through my mother eyes. She was helping me establish a path for my future – giving me real direction.

Kathy had helped me find a better apartment than the dump I rented in Chicago, decorate my place and convinced my father to pay half the rent for my studio. But I prevented myself from telling her what she'd done for me, and I was never going to accept her. After growing up the way I did, I still felt certain my mother was the victim in their hatred between each other.

During the five days I lived at home, I left in the early morning and didn't return until 11:30 each night. I just didn't want to have any contact with my mother, being too afraid of the guilt over her that I'd been raised with. I couldn't be reminded that I felt I was abandoning her. There was also the chance of actually confronting her manipulation, which was so deep inside me. I was certain it would convince me not to leave.

I didn't really say a word to my mother when I was home, except a couple sentences the second day. I left even before she said anything.

> "I won't be coming home the next three or four days until maybe 11:30 at night. I have too much work and other things to get ready for the next semester of college. I also need to see a few of my friends, who are home from school."

Each day when I came home, despite not being around my mother most of the time, I felt had been the longest five days of my life. Next Tuesday would never come soon enough.

When it finally came, I left early in the morning for my new apartment in Des Plaines. I waited until my mother left home for the grocery store, I packed just a suitcase of clothes in 10 minutes and was gone. I wasn't coming back. I had to be very discreet when I left, otherwise my will to leave could have been compromised if I'd seen my mother.

When I got in my car, I could really feel every bit of freedom. I smiled with uncontrollable emotion, clenching my hands over the steering wheel, punching the dashboard for a moment and shouting with a piercing tone. "Yes, I'm finally gone. She'll never see me again. No fuckin' way."

I thought to myself, maybe now I had the growth to change some of the deeply bitter perceptions for Kathy and my father that I couldn't do before. Hopefully the feelings since childhood would no longer follow me. I also couldn't have been more relieved that I wouldn't have to still listen to my mother's delusions, that her friends and now one of mine were spies for the Nazis.

Once I moved to my new place, I was waiting for furniture to be delivered and slept on two couch cushions for a week that Kathy gave me. I was also eating my meals using two wooden chairs, one for sitting and the other as a table for eating. She had bought them at Venture - a department store near where I lived, to use until my furniture arrived. But I didn't really care about living with nothing when I first moved into my apartment. It was saving my life – a cheap price for feeling more hopeful about my future. I realized how much the way I grew up had cost me.

My place was modernly decorated, with basic furniture – a hide-a-bed due to being a studio, a small dining room table and chairs, a new 20-inch TV, a few lamps and a coffee table. But everything was new. While my mother's home was in a nice suburb, it was older, decorated with poor taste and often disgustingly filthy. She was really cheap and didn't believe it was necessary to spend money to decorate, or clean much. We lived in filth, except the grass was cut and the snow was shoveled.

Kathy saved me from remaining in that home, my mother's spiraling trauma causing her growing paranoia and primal fear of the fate of my brother. I knew that I wouldn't have lasted, if I hadn't left.

There was no better evidence of what she did for me than looking at what my brother became living with my mother. He unquestionably was left victimized by her darkness – all the rage and hostility she left within him for my stepmother. He couldn't work any longer – not being very functional, becoming much too mentally unstable. My mother couldn't help him. How could she, with her trauma spiraling out of control?

I really feel there is a parallel between how Kathy saved me from a life that probably wouldn't have lasted and how Oskar Schindler rescued my mother, and so many other Jews, from the Nazi's atrocities. He gave them freedom, despite Europe and maybe the rest of the world, who probably felt, "People Loved Dead Jews."

My mother was transferred to work in Schindler's Emalia factory from the Plaszow concentration camp ran by Goeth – The Butcher of Plaszow. How could anyone otherwise expect what her fate would have been? If Kathy hadn't helped me leave home, with no one else there for me like she was – not even my father, I felt that I would have had a tragic destiny.

In the next few weeks, it began to feel like she was even replacing my mother, helping me to decorate my place. Or maybe she was becoming the one I never had. Kathy helped me get everything I needed - a bed, couch, kitchen table and chairs, artwork, silverware, cooking utensils, paintings and bathroom furnishings. During that time, my studio had become far more domestic and livable than I ever knew was possible growing up. As I've said, my mother's home was a filthy, embarrassing pit. Kathy had given me a taste of her elegance, style that interior decorators wish they had and being meticulous to unseen levels.

I was invited to my dad and Kathy's seven times in the next month for dinner, after I moved to my apartment in Des Plaines. I really didn't know how to interpret her becoming more involved in my life by an increasingly parental relationship. She must have saw someone who never had a mother who taught her son how to live a functional home life – one at least that was domesticated.

Despite what she had done for me, I could still be awful to her, manipulated as I was by the way I was raised by my mother. I wasn't even very conscious that my perceptions of her were always that compromised and poisoned by mother's deep bitterness. It just seemed normal to hate my stepmother.

Kathy came over to my apartment by herself one day and gave me new dishes, glasses and silverware, since I had been using paper plates and plastic forks and knives – having only lived in my place less than a week. I remember that I just wanted her to leave right after she came. I didn't say much to her when she was over and didn't thank her for everything she brought when she left. There was just a strange look of anger that covered my face she'd never seen in me before.

She didn't say much to me, or ask if anything was wrong, probably not wanting to be confrontational, seeing how I looked. I thought to myself, I'm my mother's son, and why am I agreeing to help from a woman who took my father from our family? She was raised by Nazis, who my mother told me since childhood either committed or were complicit in the atrocities against Jews in the Holocaust, including the murders of millions of them. That included my mother and her family.

One of the dinner invitations from Kathy and my father was when she cooked a traditional German dinner. The main entrée and side dishes were roasted duck, red cabbage and potato dumplings. They were delicacies of German cuisine. But while I was eating, as delicious as everything tasted, part of me felt like I was swallowing poison. I choked twice during dinner and when my stepmother asked me what was wrong, I told her I was eating more than I could chew.

My mother never would have made that dish, since she was kosher – not to mention it was a traditional German dinner, and how she despised all things German. I was conflicted and wanted to enjoy how the food tasted and tell Kathy the dishes were delicious. However, I only believed enjoying the dinner was a betrayal of my mother. If I swallowed what she cooked, I even felt that I was now one of them – a Nazi. I couldn't help but wonder if I would always have these conflicted feelings.

When I came for dinner that night Kathy was very kind to me like she had mostly been after I left home, except how dark and nasty she became anytime the conversation included my mother. We talked for a little while after we finished dinner about how when I moved into my apartment, she met me there to help me decorate and saw that I had only one suitcase of clothes. I didn't know why we had that conversation.

"Should I get the rest of my rest of my clothes, since I only packed one suitcase?" I asked.

She replied and said:

> "No, we have to get you all new things. Your mother always dressed you like you'd just moved to this country after arriving from a boat overseas in the 1940's."

> "She always complained to your father that she didn't have a dime to spend on anything better for you to wear."

> "She really had no taste, furniture, or clothes, wasn't a cook and never cleaned. Your mother didn't have gornisht (Yiddish word - meaning "nothing").

> "I can see why your father left her. She just wanted your father's money, but wouldn't spend any of it for her kids. She was not much of a mother to either of you. I don't see how your father was able to live with her for ten years."

These conversations generally hurt more than they helped, despite me believing in many respects what she said was right. It's just that it was my mother who she was viciously attacking, whom I'd lived with for close to 19 years. I still had a strong affinity for her, despite the bitter hatred she left in me and her overbearing affection at the expense of my false sense of security. How well she was able to penetrate those things inside me.

Kathy was wearing a green dress that night when I visited for dinner, the reed green worn by members of the Nazi Party which gave me nightmares growing up. I really noticed the shade of green in the dress, when she began to serve us dinner and turned towards me.

> "You've been staring at me since you've been sitting by the table. May I know why?"

"No reason," I said. "Just grateful to be invited here for dinner."

I couldn't stop fixating upon the shade of green in the color of her dress. Her dress triggered memories of my childhood, the deep fear of anyone dressed in this shade of green. I remembered my mother's stories of the Nazis' green uniforms; she mentioned them whenever she discussed the horrors inflicted upon Jews in the Holocaust. The uniforms were part of the nightmares she visualized, living through what traumatized her, particularly when talking to me of her family's fate in the Holocaust. Hearing those stories, my face turned white and I was paralyzed – maybe not even being conscious of what she was telling me.

How much I had been triggered by Kathy's dress that night. It made me remember my mother's stories of her life in the Holocaust. I was compromised – trapped with inner conflict. That night, having dinner with my stepmother, I reminded myself how pivotal Kathy's help was for me to grow, but I was convinced that I was betraying my mother.

The deepest part of the betrayal was feeling certain that I had abandoned my mother for her enemies – the triggers of eating German food and Kathy's green dress made me feel I was a Nazi, or bonding with one of them. Those feelings even recalled Nazi party ideology that I'd partly defined – Aryan supremacy being the master race of human beings, while Jews were inhuman creatures with superhuman power who had to be exterminated. Their mission was responsible for everything my mother went through and lost due during the Holocaust. How would all that guilt which rested far too deeply inside me ever change?

All those emotions inside me, which had been triggered that night also made me question again how could I have left my mother, who was suffering more than ever from her trauma, living alone with my brother? He had fallen off a cliff mentally. His illness had spiraled even more than in the past. There wasn't much left of him. He couldn't keep a job, often wound up in psychiatric hospitals – being treated with shock therapy that did nothing and lived in some of the most disgusting halfway houses when he wasn't home or in a mental institution.

But I was beginning to live a different life. I was living on my own in a modern, clean apartment. It wasn't the way I grew up in an old house, which hadn't been remodeled and was always filthy. I was also getting good grades in college and developing more of a relationship with my father and one with Kathy.

Still, what I couldn't resolve with my mother had blinded me from feeling any love for Kathy after what she'd done for me – let alone what she deserved. Just knowing, how she'd helped save me from my brother's fate, should have made me feel differently. But I couldn't change how much my mother's perceptions were mine.

My inability to express any love or even acceptance for her after all she'd done for me, probably wouldn't change without something happening that I couldn't do for myself. I didn't even know why I was so defenseless – left broken with what I couldn't move past. The inherited trauma of my mother. How could she have done that to me and my brother?

CHAPTER IV
Growth But Torn With Guilt

During my remaining three years of college, I felt Kathy and my father became the parents who replaced my mother. But maybe not. They were there for me when I left home and needed them. But my mother's overbearing affection and my devotion to her never left me. I just couldn't see them as parents after what she'd done to me.

It didn't even matter that I couldn't be around her any longer. In some ways, I just couldn't pull myself away from feeling the protection that I needed from her growing up and often being reminded when she told me that I could never leave her. I was nearly 19 when I left home, but my father and Kathy thought I was pretty undisciplined, having been raised by my mother. I wasn't a juvenile delinquent – never committed a crime, or gotten into other forms of serious trouble. But I did like to smoke pot and sometimes drank too much with my friends.

I also never cared much about how I lived or dressed until my stepmother taught me how to decorate my place and took and interest in what clothes I wore. I'd also never also worked for anyone else except my father, which I'd said was a cush job. That often happens; you get far better treated – and paid more, especially working for family than someone else. But it often doesn't help build character. Despite being in college and a business major, I also hadn't even considered what I really wanted to do when I finished. I wasn't quite ready to be on my own financially and didn't know how I would support myself if I didn't work for my father.

My father wasn't very disciplined, but Kathy practiced strong self-control due to how she was raised. Growing up in Berlin during the middle of a war, without a father despite being the youngest of seven children, her mother expected her to make her bed, help cook meals and do laundry by the time she was seven. It was a deep contrast to my mother, who I believed was enabled by her family due to their significant wealth. They had a housekeeper, so the kids only had to focus on school and religion being Orthodox.

Growing up with my mother's lenience and soft parenting, I rebelled in response to Kathy's strict parental discipline and her wanting me to do things for myself. More importantly, I felt like if I listened and adhered to her rigorous discipline, it was a deep betrayal of my mother's overbearing nurturing.

Kathy wanted my apartment to be spotless and if I ever left an unclean dish in the sink when she was there, she'd look at me with disgust. The subtle wrinkles across her forehead compressed, which almost overlapped. When I saw her facial expression, I felt that I'd seen flames. They ran across every bit of her face. I also often felt helpless not to absorb her piercing words of judgment. What she said often did more to break me down than build me up.

"What a slob you are. You're just like your mother sometimes. How did she raise you? I would have raised you differently, if you were my son."

I often didn't defend myself after she judged me like that, despite that she may have even been right. Sometimes the way I grew up, I just didn't feel good enough about myself to stand up to her. I needed to tell her there are better ways to say things to people.

How much I wasn't that clean cut kid, particularly the one Kathy wanted me to be. It couldn't have been better seen than one time with my friend Paul. He came over to my place in Desplaines one Friday afternoon in early August. We stood on the patio of my studio and smoked a joint of very latent Jamaican gangea. I became more and more stoned, being nearly visually impaired with blood-soaked red eyes.

It couldn't have been hotter and more humid that day, with sweat dripping down my face. My eyes were heavily tearing from the moisture and my hands were also wet, nearly soaked and they felt slippery as lotion. When Paul passed me the joint, I couldn't hold onto it very well.

I dropped it at least two or three times. My hands just weren't able to hold onto a rolling paper filled with pot that became increasingly smaller with each one of our tokes. The herb we smoked was also stronger than any I'd ever had before.

After Paul left, I went to Kathy and my father's home early that evening. When they answered the door, they stared at my face for what seemed like hours. I looked that stoned, being far too transparent, with a very wide grin and bloodshot eyes that triggered their disgust. Both of them didn't think that I smoked pot – let alone had ever seen me stoned. I knew they were going to let me know what they thought of me being in that condition. My stepmother didn't have any restraint in her vicious contempt for what I did. She yelled things at me that even the next-door neighbor could hear.

"How could you do this to us? Which one of your friends were you with this afternoon? I want to know who it was. I will tell your father that if he sees you like this again to no longer continue paying your rent. You can live with your mother. I don't give a shit. He'll forget you're his son."

"You know Gina Schwartz across the road is a police officer. I may call her and she'll probably arrest you.

"I never would have imagined you could do to this to both of us and yourself. Your father and I have done everything for you to have a better life in the past two years, hoping that you will be responsible. We've seen improvement, but now you're breaking our hearts. Do you even care?"

I only listened, knowing that if I tried to defend myself everything would just get really out of control. My father also didn't say much, but he looked at me with the same disgust and hostile shame that my stepmother let me know she felt.

Despite being silent, I absorbed what they said. While I didn't see my father as a parent who disciplined me, and far more not Kathy, it still mattered that they were ashamed of me. I don't know exactly why, except they were all I had now. I couldn't go back home to my mother, and I wasn't able to stand on my own yet without them.

I knew they were right in some ways by what they said. I shouldn't have shown up to their house completely stoned like that. Who knows what could have happened just driving there in that condition, let alone having them seeing me pretty screwed up. Still, I couldn't listen to them, feeling I was betraying my mother when they voiced their rage, despite telling me I'd let them down after what they'd done for me. I almost knew what my stepmother's reaction would be when I knocked on the door, knowing she was raised with unforgiving discipline by her mother after her father was murdered by the Nazis.

But I almost wanted them to see me in that condition and Kathy to know despite everything she'd done for me, I was still my mother's son. Even after she began to help me when I left I home, I've said how much I continued to see her only through my mother's eyes. Even when she was right about something, I almost had to force myself to believe she was wrong, otherwise I felt I was betraying my mother.

There was also a part of me that didn't feel what I did that day was destructive. How could I know better, being raised with the soft nurturing from my mother that was far more than tolerant, even for a child. I never had been taught discipline to study for school, going out with my friends and coming home too late, a strong work ethic, or helping take care of the house.

As long as I felt her hatred for my father and Kathy and listened to her stories of life and death in the camps during the Holocaust, that's all she ever wanted. As I've told, she still had that much influence over me, even though when I left home I felt that I'd escaped the past.

There might not have been a deeper feeling of betrayal for my mother than when I began to go with my dad and stepmother to synagogue for services on the Jewish High Holidays. I mentioned that my father didn't grow up religious and wasn't for most of his life. But my mother's family was Orthodox.

After they got married, they were only religious for a little while. But the Jewish holidays were always that important to my father. When I left home, I began to go with him and Kathy to services for the two holiest days of the year – Rosh Hashanah and Yom Kippur. He always told me why he only went to synagogue for the high holidays.

"I know that I'm not religious, but I need to attend services for the high holidays, and on Yom Kippur I fast. It lets me know that I'm still Jewish, especially growing up in forced labor camps during the Holocaust where you couldn't practice your religion."

When I began going with them to a Conservative synagogue, being there with Kathy, a German non-Jew who looked like one, I felt that I was betraying mother, and the Jewish religion. I was raised Orthodox and both my brother and I had our Bar Mitzvahs in traditional synagogues. My mother would never have let us go to temple with non-Jews, let alone being in services with my father and a Shiksa.

He never asked Kathy to convert to Judaism and I'm pretty certain she wouldn't have, since religion didn't matter very much to her. She did keep certain Jewish traditions for my father, including having a Passover seder meal, and coming with him to services for the high holidays. She loved my father and those things were really important to him.

We attended a conservative temple in West Rogers Park, Ezras Israel, and the service we went to was in the lower chapel, conducted by Rabbi Schwartzman. My father deeply loved the Rabbi. He reminded him of one of the Rabbis in his synagogue he went to once in a while with his family – as a kid living in Warsaw, before the Holocaust.

My dad used to say Rabbi Schwartzman just had great, interesting stories of life that he told for lessons of the Torah, Jewish history and moreover, meaningful ways for living our lives as Jews and just people. He said that he couldn't wait when he went to synagogue to listen to the Rabbi's stories – sitting on the edge of his seat when he told them - while growing up in Warsaw. Rabbi Schwartzman gave my father's eulogy when he passed away in 1996.

Kathy noticeably stood out when we went to services. She looked much different than the rest of the congregation. Her pretty blond hair, river blue eyes and lightly colored features were in deep contrast with our temple filled with dark-complected Sephardic and Ashkenazi Jews.

I'm certain at least the Holocaust survivors in synagogue knew she wasn't Jewish. I wondered if some even felt that she may be German. Of those, there probably were at least a few who lived with trauma like my mother's. Maybe they even thought that Kathy and her family were Nazis. I didn't react to that as much as I would have expected. I was already filled with guilt just being in temple with my father and her. I could barely call Kathy by her name when we were in synagogue – seeing her only as my father's Shiksa.

Even though the staring by other congregants at my stepmother wasn't very upsetting, I couldn't reconcile how much I felt the betrayal for my mother. I was no longer in an Orthodox temple, not even very religious anymore, and going to synagogue with my father and German stepmother. The guilt I had about being there with her, still living with my mother's trauma, had me see her at times not only as a German, but a Nazi. I was praying with the enemy of both my mother and the Jewish people.

The guilt that I betrayed my mother going to services with my father and Kathy stayed with me for the rest of my time in college. It also impacted the relationship with one of my closest friends in school, Jeff. He was Jewish and raised with conservative religious values. But somehow that was overcome, and he became my best friend for the next 20 years.

He was sort of a role model for me; studied hard, very disciplined, had good values and I loved his parents. They welcomed me like I was their son. I often ate dinner at their house. They also became my adopted family for some of the religious holidays, when I didn't go to services with my father and Kathy.

The shame that I even felt for going to synagogue with Kathy and my father reached intolerable levels one time when I came over to Jeff's house for dinner after Rosh Hashanah services. I told his parents that I had been going for a while to High Holiday services with my father and German stepmother. After I told them that, they seemed to look at me perplexed.

When their faces just glanced at me, I felt deep shame – humility, mixed with embarrassment. I didn't know if maybe it was only because Kathy wasn't Jewish – not being aligned with their conservative values, or also being German. They too might have even felt some of what my mother felt towards Germans. While I didn't know if either or both things that I said may have bothered them, I never felt more betrayal of my mother than that night with Jeff's family – telling them I was going to services with my father and stepmother. I was also real triggered by what Jeff's dad – Irving – asked me once that I wouldn't forget.

"Well, we know you grew up with strong observance for Judaism from your mother being raised Orthodox. I just wanted to ask you're going to services these days with your father and stepmother? You said she was German, but not Jewish?"

I replied and said:

"My mother and I haven't talked for a while, since I left home. It's best for now. I really couldn't stay with her any longer until she gets better."

"She's really been affected by my brother who suffered a nervous breakdown some years ago, who recovered for a while, but in the past few years his illness has spiraled."

"Yes, I'm going with my father and he wants my stepmother to go with us to services. If I want to have any family, I have to go with both of them."

Jeff's father responded by saying:

"I won't ask more about what happened with your mother. I'm not that type of person."

"Your parents are divorced, and I know that can't be easy when it comes to religious observance, particularly in Judaism."

"I was raised conservative and taught the role of family in Jewish religion is to preserve and grow the faith. Ideally, it's better when both parents are Jewish. Kathy didn't convert?"

I told Irving that she didn't, but still kept certain Jewish traditions for my father, especially coming with him to services. But I didn't say anything more to him. I was pretty triggered by what he said. Still, he wasn't saying anything another Jewish person, especially being raised conservative might have said. But after a little while, I had even become consumed with guilt, just thinking more about him telling me what the role of Jewish family is in religion. Kathy wasn't my real mother, and I was going to services with my father and his Shiksa. How was that preserving my faith? I had never felt that much betrayal of my mother after listening to what Irving asked me and said. She was raised as an Orthodox Jew.

I also had a few conversations with Jeff's grandfather, who came to America from Eastern Europe, just a few years after Hitler came into power. It almost felt like I was being unfaithful to my mother by the empathy I felt for him. He told me some of the Nazi persecution he faced, while Kathy was turning into my surrogate mother. How could I feel so much compassion for him, but still feel at times that I was betraying my mother's values and those lived with by all Jews. There were times even after I talked to him, I questioned who I was anymore, knowing how I was raised.

Jeff and his family's strong Jewish values unintentionally replenished the guilt I was beginning to slowly get over developing a relationship with Kathy. I don't believe he understood the growth she cultivated in me. What she'd done fostered my independence and personal care, including taking care of my place, teaching me how to shop and cook for myself, pay bills and care more about own hygiene. Many assume these responsibilities are a given that you learn at home from your parents while growing up. But I never did.

My mother rarely cleaned our house, since I was a child. There was dirt, soiled carpet stains everywhere and mildew that remained in our living room, bathrooms and kitchen for years. What she cooked was never appetizing, and the food in the refrigerator was generally spoiled, which she didn't mind eating. I showered once every other day, never really washed my hair or brushed my teeth much, and my toenails developed a visually disturbing fungus from bad personal hygiene.

I could never go into this extent of detail with Jeff for how I lived prior to having my own place in college. It was embarrassing telling anyone these things, let alone him. I just wanted him to think of me as being more like him or see me like anyone else. I wanted to erase my past, especially given that I felt I was taking care of myself after I left home. Maybe it wouldn't have mattered to him if he knew how I was raised.

Considering his strong religious observance, I also always felt guilty around him for establishing a relationship with Kathy – feeling that I betrayed my mother being a Holocaust survivor, who was raised Orthodox. Maybe he even saw my father being with Kathy as a betrayal of the Jewish faith. But I really couldn't tell the difference of whether this was what I was projecting on him due to my guilt or something that actually bothered him.

Jeff had been a very good student, and I'd said had very disciplined studying habits in college. It really rubbed off on me. He told me some of that was due to not having a stronger commitment to school when he was growing up, which impacted his grades. His interests were heavily related to music, and he was in a few bands in high school. He may have even told me that his only ambition in high school was to be a rock star. His change to focusing on school in college was probably realizing - and his parents telling him - the odds of being a famous musician were just a real longshot and maybe pure luck.

My mother as I've told was not any help for me with discipline for studying in school. She never really had taken much of an interest in what I was learning. But I probably shouldn't have expected anything more due to how much she went through. She could only focus on herself.

In college, my grade point average was strong, consistently a B to B+ average, but I really didn't know what I wanted to do. I changed my major so many times during my first two years of college. I switched from business communications to management, economics, behavioral consumption and finally marketing, since it was an easier academic curriculum for business than some other majors. But Kathy thought marketing wasn't best for my skills. She felt that I might not be able to find a job that paid well when I graduated. What she'd said convinced me to change my major from marketing to finance at the end of my sophomore year.

> "I know you like to talk, you're good at math and like to talk about investments, which are all skills and interests that I've heard help you in finance to find a good career."

> "You'll have a job probably before you leave college or when you graduate. I'm certain it will pay better than other fields, and I've heard there are more opportunities the others you've considered."

> "Let's not burden your father with having to continue to support you when you graduate. Hasn't he helped you enough financially?

> "He's done much more than a father would ever do for his son. He's paid your college, helped pay your rent and you make very good money working for him. Both of us really saved you when you left home."

After I heard what Kathy said, I felt it was the advice I needed for my future. I needed direction as to what I wanted to do after I graduated. What she told me was very practical, clear and an awakening honestly. It was truly convincing to lead me in a path towards my future. How could I not want to do things that I was good at and liked to do?

I just wished that when she helped me, I didn't feel she kept score for everything that her and my father did for me. It made me at times even resent her more the way I was raised – growing up with that much hatred for her, despite it was never deserved.

Kathy was right due to what she told me and changed my major. . In less than a month after I graduated, I was hired by Motorola for their Risk Analysis team in the company's Cellular Technology division. My salary was far greater than many business graduates with other majors. Her direction had let me find a path for myself. It was a real future when I didn't know what I wanted to do. But I couldn't even thank her for what she'd done. While she'd pointed me to the right field for my career, I just couldn't accept, or feel much towards her – not after everything I heard from my mother growing up. I remained trapped by what she'd done to me. I still couldn't feel about Kathy any differently.

My mother couldn't have given me what she did in helping me find a career with strong potential. Growing up in Krakow, with Kristallnacht beginning in 1938 when my mother was 13, there was no longer any opportunity for a Jew to have an education. You were only hoping that you'd be lucky enough to survive during the Holocaust.

Kathy had finished high school and was not traditional like my mother. I've mentioned that her appearance when your eyes turned towards her was stunning, more modern and elegant than most – and she was well-informed, obsessed with being abreast of the world. Given her understanding of life in the present, unlike my mother, it's not surprising that she was pivotal for helping me find a career where I could flourish.

In my junior year of college, my life continued to improve. I moved from my apartment in Des Plaines to a newly built apartment complex in Wheeling. It was only 10 minutes away from my father and Kathy's townhouse in Deerfield. I was now much closer to them than my place in Des Plaines. The rent was more expensive than my studio, but my stepmother saw this being a way to improve my quality of life, with a nicer place being very close to them. She was taking more of an active interest in my well-being than I'd ever expected. I became even more of what she wanted me to be.

Cleanliness and living in a newly built apartment building were even more important to me than when she first opened my eyes to a different life after I left home. I'd said that I also began to cook for myself and always had fresh food in my refrigerator. My mother probably no longer would have recognized me.

I couldn't even remember how I lived with my her once I moved into my new place. After I left home, I often blamed her. Sometimes it even led to feeling hostility that she didn't care how we lived. But how could I have seen it differently? It was like her kids didn't matter. I never brought any friends to our house. I felt they'd feel I was strange if they'd seen the filth all over the place. But it often didn't bother me living that way being raised how I was. As I grew older, I often felt the way we lived was probably even unsanitary.

I remember once having a conversation with my father and stepmother when I visited their home when I lived in my new apartment. My father asked me if I missed my mother.

> "Why? I couldn't live that way any longer. Nothing in the house had been cleaned in years – the carpets, the floors and the toilets had rings that were soiled. The food in our refrigerator was often spoiled and my mother had become really fuckin crazy."

He didn't reply, or Kathy. But I don't know if that was what they wanted to hear. They had no reason to want me to think about her differently. But I felt Kathy, despite far too many years of bitterness between them had some compassion for my mother. Maybe just knowing that she lost a large family, being only a kid is why she may have felt that away. But I was certain my father didn't have any sympathy for my mother. How could he? He never loved her and hated her, not even long after they were married.

Despite all the positive changes that Kathy cultivated in me, I was still conflicted and often felt my growth wasn't even deserved. How could that be any different – knowing how much I felt compromised that I abandoned my mother when I left home? I just couldn't forget how I was raised.

While I still saw my growth that she helped me realize, I didn't know what it would take for me to see her differently. There was nothing I could do that would change how I felt; I needed help, but didn't know where, or who it would come from. My mother wasn't going to change and while my father didn't do this to me, I too often looked at him with some of the same rage that I had for my stepmother.

I didn't even think about seeking professional help. I felt my hatred was normal, and in the early 1980's there was such a stigma about mental health. But I never really told my stepmother how I felt, knowing that I couldn't lose her, seeing everything that she was doing for me. She and my father also had become my family. I hadn't talked to my mother in nearly two years.

But there were times Kathy just triggered me. I would voice every bit of my feelings of resentment toward her, especially when she criticized my mother. She'd always respond when I told her what I felt. It was way more vicious than what I said to her. But it seemed like it was more so her defensively reacting.

One night, I went over to their house for dinner and my clothes weren't as clean as Kathy wanted. There were a few spots on my shirt and pants and my leather shoes were a bit scratched. It wasn't anything really disgusting, but that's not the way she felt.

> "Let's not be like your mother who doesn't care about her appearance. You've grown so much, don't go back to what you left."

I replied with:

> "You can't say these things to me. You're not my mother and you never will be. I can't believe you don't have more sympathy for her, knowing what she went through. You didn't lose what she did. I really can't stand when you tell me what to do all the time. She never would."

Kathy said:

> "How can you defend your mother? You know what she did to you, not to mention how she destroyed your brother. You know what I went through with your father all these years.".

> "She did everything possible to ruin us and that will never happen. I'm not criticizing you when I say these things. They're only to help you improve yourself."

> "I want what is best for you. I don't think your mother ever did."

I didn't say anything more after what she told me. I had said what I wanted to and heard what she said. While I agreed with most of it, I still was pretty hurt by what she said. When I heard Kathy tell me pretty nasty things about my mother, I always questioned if she would have been any different, going through what my mother did. She grew up without a father and had to live through the most dehumanizing war in history. But how could it be even measurable to what happened to my mother.

I knew she was right about much of what she said, but I had to defend my mother because of the way she brought me up. I couldn't react differently. The commitment I had to her rested that deeply inside me, but for some of the wrong reasons. It was always her manipulation that manifested in smothering affection and overprotection. That too often strangled me. But I always had to defend her when Kathy or my father attacked her – being left to only see them through her eyes.

I'd lived in my new apartment in Wheeling for nearly eight months and one night there was a phone call from my mother. I really didn't know what to say to her and panicked when I answered. I was shocked and didn't know how she would've gotten my phone number. It wasn't even listed. She said to me "Bobby, is that you?" It was something you'd normally expect someone to say when they called. But I didn't want to ever have anything to do with her after I left home, and my nerves were uncontrollable.

My heart was beating louder and faster than gunshots firing in rapid succession. My face became tense – feeling harder than a log falling off a tree. I also felt my jaw dropping, like it had nearly fallen to the floor. I hadn't talked to my mother for two and a half years since I left home. She never had the phone number where I lived until that day.

When I answered the phone, I didn't say a word for several minutes. Neither did she, but then told me how deeply she missed me, couldn't love anyone more and needed to know when I was coming home. She said she couldn't be without me. I lost it and shouted at her with unseen rage.

"Don't Call Me Ever Again!!"

I violently slammed the receiver into the wall mount for the phone hanging on the kitchen wall. There was a ringing sound that I couldn't get out of my ears for a couple hours that night due to how hard I hit the receiver against the wall.

The rest of the night, I couldn't stop worrying, knowing my mother had my phone number and might call me again. What means could she have used to get my number? I was that afraid she would call me again and somehow just like the past I'd be controlled by her. It would be no different than when I was a child growing up. I'd go back to my former self and the life before I left home.

I was also obsessed that if she had my number, she'd know where I lived and come over. I had to remind myself that she wasn't presently anywhere near me. Since I had an unlisted number, eventually I realized there wasn't any way she could know my address. What I said to myself seemed to calm me down that night, but I still panicked at times for nearly a week.

My fear of hearing from her again became real two weeks after she called me. She and my brother showed up in the parking lot of my apartment complex in Wheeling. When I noticed them, I panicked and began to sweat until my shirt was soaked. My heart was also vibrating uncontrollably. I instinctively hid below the window frame so they couldn't see me. I also turned off the lights. They didn't know which apartment I lived in the building. I hoped they'd think I wasn't home and leave.

But somehow, they had the address where I lived, except the building's front door was locked and my name wasn't listed next to the door leading into the building. They rang the doorbells for all eight apartments of my building, since they didn't know my unit number. I didn't answer, still hiding underneath my living room window. I shivered with fear – feeling nearly paralyzed from the doorbells ringing for the apartments continuously. They sounded like bells in a carnival arcade, being rung for winning prizes by firing gunshots nearest to the bullseye.

After 10 minutes, the numbing sounds of the doorbells stopped and my mother and brother left the parking lot and drove away. I couldn't have been more relieved, and my heart no longer felt like it was pounding too loudly, feeling like a bomb ticking ready to detonate. But they knew where I lived, and I had to accept that they might come back. If they would, I was still certain that I wouldn't act any differently than how I did.

I hadn't seen my mother for over two years and I couldn't have been more triggered by my guilt for not having talked to her for that long. Even more triggering at times, I felt the betrayal in developing a relationship with Kathy. As I'd told, the latter was my mother's deeper fear – not only that I would leave her, but that someday I would turn against her and side with my stepmother. I've said it's why I felt she gave me that much spending money when I went away to college – letting me feel that I still couldn't live without her.

When I saw my brother in the parking lot, it was the first time I'd really thought of him since I left home. The thoughts of him triggered memories I'd forgotten of how he attacked my stepmother once verbally and another time viciously. While he didn't physically assault her the first time, what happened was still heartbreaking and I'm certain it never left him.

Harry told me a few times what he'd done when he assaulted Kathy verbally and physically in the ways he did. It tore him up. He felt that he needed to do what he did because of how much he hated my stepmother, especially when my mother told us that "the Daichke-whore took your father from me and you kids." Still, he felt possessed by what he'd done. Even with his hatred for my stepmother, he often couldn't believe what he did to her. He never could really understand why he attacked her in the ways that he did.

I'm not certain whether my mother forced him to commit both of the assaults – one when he was 15 and the other at 16. But if not, she was still responsible for what happened because of how much her hatred influenced him. Both of the attacks were told to me by my brother, when he was home for a while before he went back to a halfway house.

I was in shock after what he told me, but anything was possible with my mother. All her rage after everything that happened to her meant that she had to blame someone – why not my German stepmother and every other German? She convinced us both, but destroyed my brother telling us Kathy was our bitter enemy when we were kids. As I've told, I was five, when my mother first began to inflict those feelings of hatred in me. She began to do that to Harry, when he was 10. It was right after my dad left her. He was 10 years older than me, as I'd mentioned. What she did, just impacted him far more than me growing up.

Both the assaults happened when my dad lived in an apartment with my stepmother in the city next to the lakefront in East Rogers Park by Evanston. Their place was nearly 30 minutes away from our home in West Rogers Park and each one happened later at night. When I knew the effort my brother put in, driving back and forth pretty far, and that both attacks had been late at night, I felt he was obsessed with hostility. He didn't see any other way to defend my mother.

The first one was near 10:30 PM on a warm night in mid-summer. My brother drove to my father's apartment, walked in the building and rang his doorbell incessantly – maybe 30 or 40 times – but my stepmother didn't answer. She could see through the camera in her apartment that he was in their building and wasn't leaving. But Kathy talked to my brother for a minute and then decided to let him upstairs.

"Harry, what is it that you want? It's after 10:30 and your father has to get up for work early tomorrow morning."

He replied and said:

"I just want to talk to you for a minute. I'm not doing well today and having a hard time with school. I just want to see my father. My mother really can't help me."

After listening to him, she pushed the buzzer for him to come upstairs. He rode the elevator to my father's apartment on the 10th floor, feeling more hostile by the second, not even knowing what he would say to her. He was remembering the infested hatred from my mother that had penetrated every bit of him.

"The Daichke's family were Nazis. They helped take my family away from me when they were murdered in Auschwitz and Belzac. She took my husband and your father from us, knowing you're only kids. She's German filth, who isn't human."

"Stay away from her, but if you see that bitch, tell her what she did to us and everything that her family did to me."

After Harry stepped out of the elevator, he walked quickly, telling me that he felt uncontrollable rage and was obsessed with purpose getting closer to my father's door. He knocked loudly, maybe three or four times. One of the neighbors heard him, opened their door for a minute to see who was out there and then went back into their apartment. When Kathy answered, my brother didn't let her say a word. He was filled with hostility and tears.

"How were you able to do what you did to us? My mother's a victim and what about me and my little brother? My father left us for you when she was pregnant with Bobby.

"Who could do this to someone? It just can't be real that a German, whose family were Nazis, is married to my father. He's Jewish, not to mention a Holocaust survivor."

"You can't even begin to know what that has done to my mother. How much she has suffered and lost."

"She has nothing left. Her family is gone and she has no husband. You have my dad and your family. My mother only has me and my little brother. We never even see our father much."

"That's because when he isn't working, he's always with you. Why did you take him from us? How do you live with yourself?"

Then Harry spit in her face and my father pushed him away from the door. When he heard my brother's voice and listened to what he told Kathy, he rushed from the bedroom to where she was standing. She didn't say a word to my brother after what he said. But she looked at him ready to explode with her vicious temper. Then she raised her hand wanting to slap him in the face.

Kathy was never one to hide her emotions and had rage herself about many things, especially when she was being attacked by someone. Maybe it was just the way she grew up. Even though she was German, she probably felt sometimes that she had to defend herself in a war where you were never certain what could happen to you. It didn't even matter who you were sometimes. I've said she was also raised in the Holocaust without a father, despite six other brothers and sisters to take care of her. How could she have grown up differently?

My father reflexively pulled Kathy's hand back when she was going to slap my brother. I'm certain knowing my father, the hostility seen in his face made it seem like he might even kill my brother.

"Get the hell out of here now, you mother fucking piece of shit. Never come back here again, or to anywhere else I may live. Otherwise, I don't know what I may do to you."

My brother was silent and left covered in tears after what my father said, running to the elevator and to his car after he left the building. He was filled with rage and fear driving home that night. What he said to my stepmother triggered fresh scars of the hatred my mother had raised him to feel, while being frozen with relentless fear – and heartbroken since he didn't know whether he'd even see my father again.

He came that home night after driving in his car awhile – maybe wanting to understand what he'd done. But I don't think he really could, since my mother's control over his thoughts probably made him feel that what he did was nothing more than defending her. He was that powerless.

By the time Harry came home, it was nearly 1:30 AM. He had been gone for three and a half hours to carry out my mother's wishes. But he didn't expect there might be unforeseen costs. When he came in the house, my mother saw that his face looked redder than blood and covered with dried tears. He told her he did what she wanted, but that he might never see his father again. I guess he didn't consider t h a t my father would react the way he did. But he realized what happened might tear their relationship apart.

While my mother didn't actually tell Harry to go over to my father's house and attack Kathy, it's what he felt he had to do. He needed to let her feel every bit of my mother's hatred for her. She asked him, what he did. "I asked the Deichke something I always heard you say, Why did you take our father and your husband from us?" He didn't say anything else and just went to bed. He didn't want to answer any more of her questions, maybe knowing that he'd regret what he'd done.

Despite what my father said to my brother, and that he probably never wanted to see him again, he knew what happened was something beyond his control. He knew how damaged he was by my mother's uncontrollable hatred. I've said, my brother was 10, but I had just been born when my father left my mother. He'd also been raised in their tortured marriage. I can't say enough, the hatred she left in him just had to sit far deeper than in me. He was much older than I was, being only a baby. It made him an easy target to be uncontrollably impacted by what she did to us.

After my father told him not to come back to his house, they didn't talk for a few months. But eventually, with time and probably understanding that my brother couldn't control what he did, they began talking again.

My dad wasn't innocent in his hatred for my mother, which also often controlled him. But it was nothing comparable to what she did to us. What else could you expect from a marriage that over time took no prisoners, a divorce with no regret for the other, and two children who were in the middle of their parents' crisis?

The second assault by my brother wasn't until six months later. Harry knew that Kathy wouldn't answer the door again, if he came over without my father home. What happened was still fresh in her mind. But it made him far more clever in what he did the first time. He discreetly parked his car near the garbage dumpsters of my father's apartment building for a week to find out if Kathy regularly took out the garbage at a certain time. He determined it was always the same time every Monday, Wednesday and Thursday night, near 8:00.

On a freezing cold Thursday night in December, my brother waited for Kathy to throw out the garbage. It was a little later for her than usual – maybe 8:30. He knew my father wouldn't be home that night until much later, since he was playing cards with his friends. After he saw her near the dumpster he ran from his car. She put the garbage bag she was holding down and looked at him in shock.

> "What are doing you here? If your father was here, I don't know what he would do to you. I'll call the police, if you move one step closer. I don't care what they to do you."

He moved forward towards her, grabbed her neck and pulled her hair until she was screaming and wouldn't stop crying when he yelled in her face.

> "How does it feel? I have to torture you. You need to know what my mother and her family went through in the Holocaust. It's what your family and the rest of the Nazis did to them."

My brother was pulling Kathy's hair with such rage that he wasn't even conscious of what he was doing. Incredibly, he didn't pull any hair out of her head. She defended herself a bit as best she could – only able to slap his face once or twice. But then she was overpowered by him, when he grabbed both her hands and pulled them away from his face. He reflexively assaulted her – reacting to every moment of my mother's uncontrollable hatred and disgust for my stepmother. He acted with vicious contempt due to how he was raised – a mechanism for her malice.

When Harry actually attacked her it wasn't for that long. It lasted for only five or six minutes. But he panicked after what he'd done. He felt someone had to have seen what happened and looked for a second to see whether he'd seen anybody. Then he ran to his car, or more like sprinted faster than he ever felt he could. He was mixed with vengeance and tears for what he'd done. It was no different than the first time he attacked her.

He drove home right after what happened, heavily conflicted by anger and fear. He came in the house, my mother saw the way he looked and asked him where he'd gone. He told her to his father's, but she didn't ask why. He didn't wait long and told her everything he did to Kathy, being smothered with the emotions he felt after attacking her.

> "Just like last time, I did what you wanted me to do to his Shiksa. I don't know what my father will do to me, when she tells him."

My mother's response had no emotion – regret, compassion, or any sensitivity. She only felt it was some revenge that was needed for what she went through, or at least a little justice. But like the first time, she hadn't told my brother to attack Kathy. Still it didn't make any difference, being filled with so much hatred for her that he couldn't control it any longer. He was just doing what he felt my mother needed but couldn't do herself. She even told him that justice had been done.

> "The Deichke got what she deserved, for what her family and the rest of the Nazis did to me and my family in the Holocaust. She also took your father from me, you and Bobby. Don't worry about him, I'll take care of everything."

When my father learned what happened that night, he called my mother early the next morning. He talked to her only for a couple minutes. Then he hung up the phone before she could say very much.

> "I won't call the police and tell them what happened, since one way or the other you put Harry up to this. You are nothing but fucking vicious, nasty and resentful."

> "You think you're the only one who's suffered. How could I have even stayed with you for as long as I did?"

> "Rose, listen to what I am telling you, if he does anything, anything to her again, I don't know what I'll do to you."

She replied and said,

> "If you think I'm afraid of you, I'm not."

My father responded and said,

> "Just remember what I told you. If I have to, I'll destroy you. You don't know what I can do."

There was no way to justify what my brother did to Kathy, except that both assaults were maybe the best examples of how far my mother's vengeance for Kathy penetrated within my brother. I've felt both of them were pivotal for him to lose his mind.

But when I was older, I questioned why the trauma we inherited had to happen. It was a few years after learning how Kathy's father was murdered. But it was too late to change Harry's perceptions and no longer would meaningfully change mine. How could I not repeatedly ask; Why didn't we know growing up that a Nazi German saved my mother's life and that my stepmother's father wasn't a Nazi? If only we could have known the truth back then.

Once some time passed, a few years after my brother attacked Kathy, my father let him begin to come over to his house again. Another factor probably in his decision was knowing that what happened Harry hadn't done by his own will. He knew it was something my mother would have wanted him to do.

He came to see my dad one day when he and Kathy still lived in their East Rogers Park apartment near the lakefront. He talked to them for a few minutes and my stepmother told him that she wanted to give him something. She stood in front of Harry, opened a small white jewelry box and gave him a gold Jewish "Star of David," with a necklace. He decided to wear the gift right after she gave it to him and thanked her repeatedly. He was shocked that she was giving him anything, let alone a Star of David – after what happened and knowing that he often only referred to her as a Shiksa or the Deichke. She also knew that he felt certain some of her family were Nazis.

Kathy thought the gift would let them begin to at least get to know each other. I guess she felt enough time had passed after what happened to feel a bit safer with him. Maybe she also wanted to begin to offer forgiveness - knowing that he couldn't have probably asked for it himself by the way he was raised.

Harry was smiling when he came home later that evening, near 10:00. He was still wearing the gift from my stepmother. He began to feel that maybe Kathy wasn't everything my mother said. She wasn't asleep yet and instantly saw what he was wearing. The Star of David was pulled over his shirt, hanging down maybe five or six inches from the necklace my stepmother gave him around his neck.

My mother questioned where he got it multiple times. But my brother was deeply shaking when she confronted him – being that scared of her. Finally, he told her the gift was from Kathy. She told him to take off the necklace and give it to her before he left the room. He initially refused, but finally feeling heartbroken by what she said and covered in tears, he gave her the gift. Probably with never more rage, she yelled at him with no restraint.

"If I ever see you wearing that again, don't come home. The Deichke took your father from us and you know what her family might have even did to mine."

He didn't reply and his face looked insanely hostile; maybe he wanted to beat up my mother. But rather, he ran out of the house that night, nearly drowning in tears, and didn't return home until the next morning. They didn't talk for nearly three weeks after he came home.

I remembered only some of what happened that night, being eight and mostly asleep in my bedroom. My brother also told me the story a few months after learning from him about both the attacks of Kathy. He told me that he was pretty certain my mother didn't even try to find him or call anyone after he left to see where he'd gone. I guess her rage for my stepmother overcame being worried about the way he left and where he might have gone

After just hearing what my mother did, thinking about how he must have felt, it probably messed him up even more than what he did to Kathy. I was consumed with guilt by what I heard. How could I have survived and gone through what he did? While I suffered as well, also living with every bit of my mother's hatred, I can't say enough, it wasn't what happened to him.

My brother paid deeply for both times he attacked Kathy, being that controlled by mother. But any hope for beginning to see her differently was gone when my mother took away her gift to him. I'm certain after what she said when he came home, he felt that he'd betrayed her by accepting the gift. But despite also being enraged at what she told him, he couldn't separate himself from his hatred for my stepmother. How else would my mother want him to feel?

The things that I've mentioned that happened to Harry, in some ways were a blessing for me. It let me eventually see that while my mother had suffered more than was human, her kids were like instruments to channel her emotions, especially my brother. As I've told, I often felt she didn't care about us; it was only her suffering and losses. She was a victim, but so were we. That couldn't have been clearer than a brother who didn't survive what she did to him. How could a mother do what she had done to her children? I needed to remember that to overcome some of the guilt that I felt after I left home, especially due to the relationship I'd formed with Kathy.

But feeling that my brother and I were victims, I knew it wouldn't last. I couldn't see Kathy much differently than my mother due to what she wanted me too believe, that began as a child. Still if only seeing what Harry had gone through couldn't change how I felt, was there anything that ever would?

It was getting near the end of my final semester in college, and I was interviewing for other jobs before I was offered the position with Motorola. In that final couple of months, I often dwelled on whether it was in my best interest inviting my mother to the graduation. I couldn't invite my brother, he was no longer mentally stable. It's not that I wanted my mother there, but was conflicted by guilt. She was still my mother, and I knew how I was raised. But I questioned why I needed to invite her – knowing she'd never helped me with college.

It was Kathy that had led me to a major that gave me a real future, being offered a great job right after I graduated. I hadn't talked to my mother for four years and we were estranged. Love or even respect wasn't my motivation to consider inviting her. It was just how much guilt that she wanted me to feel over her growing up. But despite the emotions, it didn't change my decision to not invite her.

I wish that I could have thanked Kathy for how much she helped me in college after I left home. She not only led me to my major, but told me repeatedly – if I didn't get good grades, I'll graduate but not get a good job. There were times before an exam when I mentioned to her that I've studied what I need to know, but if I just pass it's enough. She reminded me that wasn't what I should only want, saying "You have to get a job when you graduate to support yourself. You can't continue to work for your father after college. He doesn't want you to depend on him anymore." The last few things she said didn't even bother me very much. I knew that I couldn't depend on my father anymore and needed to actually stand on my own.

I had never even given her any credit for my 3.0/3.2 overall GPA and in my major. Loyola University, the college I attended was also a well-respected business school. It was a prominent name. But none of this could have happened, if I hadn't left home. It let Kathy give me what I needed. As I've said I had to leave. It was my only way to survive – knowing how much my mother's condition had spiraled and that probably otherwise I would have wound up like my brother.

CHAPTER V

On My Own –
But Detachment Not Yet Found

I graduated from college in January 1985 and the ceremony was at the Hotel Marriott in downtown Chicago. It was not typical weather for a graduation ceremony being in the heart of winter. I'd skipped one semester after I was late for enrollment the second half of my freshman year. But I still felt fortunate when I finished – graduating only one semester later than expected. I probably never would have even gone back to college, if I hadn't left home – let alone that I probably wouldn't have survived not to be away from my mother and brother.

As I was waiting for my name to be read to walk up and receive my diploma, I knew that not only Kathy and my father came to the ceremony, but also my mother and brother. He had been in a psychiatric hospital right before I graduated. I guess somehow he begged my mother to come home and she let him. While I didn't invite them, knowing my mother she probably called the college, told them I was her son and that there probably was a mistake why she and my brother weren't sent an invite.

My mother was relentless when she was determined to find something out. It's how she got more alimony from my father than he wanted to pay her. When they were getting divorced, she told her attorney that my father wasn't reporting all of the earnings from his business, as they were negotiating their divorce settlement. After her lawyer hired an accountant to review his tax returns, he knew that my father included some personal expenses within his business to reduce the company's earnings. He did that so he could pay my mother less alimony than would have been required to pay her.

Once I knew that my mother and brother had come to the ceremony, I felt the same anxiety as when I saw them in the parking lot of my apartment in Wheeling and at my high school graduation. My stomach was full of knots, which felt like steel weights inside me – and my pulse seemed like it was running faster and beating louder than a train speeding uncontrollably.

My heart also wouldn't stop pounding, like the train's wheels were riding that heavily over the tracks. I didn't want them to be there. As I've mentioned, my mother didn't do anything to help me get through college. How much I resented her – knowing that I also probably wouldn't have done anything with my life if I hadn't left home.

But as I've told, I felt guilty about not inviting her to my graduation. Despite her overbearing affection growing up, she protected me, even though it was far too much. I couldn't have remembered that more than being constantly picked on when I was a kid for being fat. While she didn't help me with my classes had still wanted me to get passing grades. I sometimes felt that I owed her for even getting me to finish high school, not having had much of an interest in school. I guess that I could understand why I felt guilty for not inviting her. But I've said, it was Kathy who pushed me to succeed in college.

The direction that she gave me I've often felt had parallels in some ways to how Oskar Schindler sacrificed himself and everything he had to save Jewish lives in the Holocaust. It certainly wasn't the same as what he did to rescue every Jewish life he could, after his feelings towards Jews changed. But Kathy was able to leave behind all the years of my hatred for her. She gave me real hope when no one else was there. Somehow she detached herself from what she must have felt to help me become someone. Otherwise, I can't say enough how I don't know what would have happened to me.

I had many job interviews prior to my graduation, but the rejection letters didn't deter me from obtaining the position with Motorola. The formal offer came a month after I graduated, but I was pretty certain they'd hire me after my third interview a few weeks before then. Once I accepted the position, I rented a new apartment in a luxury high rise with my best friend from high school, Scott. The new place was in a recently gentrified neighborhood of Chicago – North Uptown – with a balcony overlooking the beach and lakefront. I felt that fulfilled having a job in the profession of my major and no longer needing my father's financial support.

Despite that I'd been rejected for many positions, Kathy would always tell me, "you have to keep going." I also remembered my dad's past of never giving up when he came to America after the Holocaust. I've said that he overcame five businesses that failed before the sixth venture flourished. It helped me never get discouraged.

But when I obtained the offer from Motorola, as excited I was, I couldn't acknowledge Kathy nearly as much as she deserved for what she'd done for me. How often I wasn't even aware of the disgust for her that I often felt. It really had penetrated every bit of me.

I also became convinced that I didn't really need her anymore. I was able to support myself and had become pretty domesticated. But as I'd said, probably most of that wouldn't have happened without her. Still even feeling that I no longer needed anything from her, would that be sustainable? Would there

Schindler saving Jewish lives didn't begin as a personal crusade. The atrocities he'd seen committed against Jews in Plaszow and the Krakow ghetto were a turning point in transforming him from exploiting Jews to saving them. But I learned how to bitterly hate Kathy as a child. How could I change how I was raised? Would she be there for me again if I needed her?

As I've told, I didn't necessarily even see the hatred – to me it was normal. What I'd known since childhood probably wouldn't be something that I could change. The feelings about Kathy were too deep inside me.

I was excited starting my position with Motorola. I was no longer working for my father, though I was nervous to work for someone else. In my first year there, I came into the office at 7:00 – two hours before anyone else – and generally left at 6:00, an hour after most people had gone. It was generally a 50 to 60-hour work week, more than the required 40 hours. I felt I had to overcompensate to do my job effectively, since I'd never worked for anyone except my father.

After being with them for about a year and a half, I left work one day and suddenly starting to think about my brother again and everything that happened to him. I couldn't stop remembering how much he was impacted by my mother, but also panicked about why the same thing couldn't happen to me. I was a different person than him, but survivor guilt began to compromise my thinking.

There was one time at work I was writing a report that was due early the next morning. But I couldn't stop questioning everything I was doing. Why am I working on the report? What was its purpose, why did I even have a job? But most importantly, I questioned why I deserved to live differently than my brother? I had a comfortable apartment, with a job that paid well, while my brother had turned into a vegetable. I was obsessed to answer one question – Why couldn't his fate also have been mine? I'd become traumatized with that guilt.

I questioned why I felt that was no longer conscious of how much I'd grown. Why could I no longer see that my life wasn't my brother's? I felt defenseless, a victim not able to recognize how much more my mother controlled him than me. I can't say enough how much more he'd been damaged than I was. But I just wasn't able to control what was happening.

Still my will and mind were unquestionably stronger than my brother's. I counteracted my thoughts by telling myself that I wasn't mentally dysfunctional. I needed that much reassurance to confront my survivor guilt that I was sane and not my brother. When I even had the irrational thoughts, I would compulsively tell myself things like I had a good job, lived on my own and had a healthy social life. It helped me rewire how I was thinking.

But there were times that I didn't think about what was haunting me and couldn't have been more relieved. Though it was purely temporary, waiting for those thoughts to return. There just had to be something that would help me move past what I was going through.

I didn't know why this insanity was happening to me. Maybe it was a justifiable reaction to my repressed guilt. The feelings of having abandoned my mother and my brother when they were mentally spiraling. But part of me still knew I only left home since I couldn't stay – realizing their fate also threatened my survival.

There were times I even felt in crisis for what I was going through and that I wouldn't recover. I often couldn't see how these thoughts would ever end. I only coped but temporarily – needing to repeatedly convince myself that I wasn't my brother.

The turning point didn't come until nearly three months after my breakdown, when the functional values my stepmother helped me cultivate had permanently made a difference. I reminded myself that the luxury apartment that I lived in by the lakefront and a healthy social life couldn't have been a deeper contrast to the filthy, often unsanitary conditions and psychologically unhealthy environment I lived with in my mother's house. I came to realize again that Harry was mentally ill, but I wasn't, while my mother was facing her own psychological crisis.

During the time I was spiraling, my roommate Scott mentioned my mother called me one afternoon and asked if I was home. Fortunately, I wasn't. It shouldn't have mattered, since I wouldn't have felt any different than when she called my apartment in Wheeling. But I panicked when I even knew she called. It was the same as what happened last time. When I heard her name, I wanted to run somewhere far, where she'd never find me. This was the only way that I felt I could erase her from my mind.

I didn't know how my mother found my phone number. It was unlisted and I wanted it the same as the other places I'd lived. It couldn't be different, if I wanted to keep my life. After leaving home, I had always been that afraid if I even talked to her that I might come back to what I ran from when I left. I might feel that guilty for leaving her when she needed me and sometimes I asked Scott what my mother wanted when she called.

"She asked to talk to you and questioned why I wouldn't put you on the phone. You weren't home," he said. He thought that she didn't believe him.

I replied and said:

"She'll never call here in the future. I'll make sure of it."

"Okay, I hope not. I never met her, but the way she thought I was lying that you weren't home, I felt was strange," he said.

The last few things he said weren't surprising. When I was a teenager, I'd always come to his house after school. But he never came to mine. Rarely any of my friends came over. I often asked him if I could stay a little while longer when I was over, despite knowing that his family ate dinner between 5:00 – 6:00. The excuse I would tell him for not leaving was my mom wasn't home and I didn't know if she'd cooked dinner. But I never told him that I was ashamed of how I lived. Still I became used to it by how I was raised. Our house was nothing like Scott's. His home was much newer than our place built in the early 1940's, decorated well and that clean you often felt like you could eat off the floor. Whenever I introduced my friends to my mother, she would also ask crazy questions that would generally embarrass me in some way. He must have known that since I never invited him over, there were some things I just didn't want him to know.

One time I did invite my friend Larry to my house, when I was about 16. My mother just stood by the door when he came in and stared at him for 20 minutes, but she didn't say a word. Larry asked me what she was doing, and he didn't understand why she couldn't stop looking at him. I told him my mother had been impacted by something my brother did and she'd be okay. But I was lying and pretty certain that she panicked, silently reacting to paranoia from what was becoming uncontrollable Holocaust trauma. There were times I saw her like this with her friends. I knew that from some really strange conversations with her. It's when she told me that they were Nazi spies.

I said that my mother often thought some of her friends and my friend Mike when I was older were members of the Line, which finally made me leave home. She said that they were spies, who would let the Gestapo know where she was hiding for being deported to a concentration camp. My face shriveled and was embarrassed watching her stare at Larry, convinced that's what she was thinking about him. I had to come up with something quickly when I told him what she was doing. How would I explain to him what was happening to her?

When my mother called me at home, I'd said that I felt like I did when I lived in my apartment in Wheeling. I became even more afraid than back then that she might come over unexpectedly. What would I do then? I now had a roommate. How would I explain to him that I couldn't see her. We hadn't talked in five years.

But at least my building had a doorman. He wouldn't let her come up to my apartment, if I told him not to. I was just frantic that she would make a scene and not leave. I'd be forced to call the police on my own mother. How would I not be embarrassed having to explain that to Scott – or telling that to anybody else I knew in the building, if they had seen something.

It's shocking I felt that afraid of my mother, despite living on my own the past five years. The more panicked I became hearing that she called, the more it helped me remember everything she did to my brother. It was the rage I felt for how she helped ruin his life, which let me see the unforgettable trauma that no one should have had to have gone through – not him or me. I was blind to every bit of hatred I inherited, but thinking of my mother triggered seeing how much my brother was impacted. With that understanding and how clearly I differentiated my life from my brother's, I was finally able to recover from the crisis that I'd been confronted with in my mind.

A few weeks after I recovered from my breakdown, I was driving my car on a Saturday morning in early March. I was near my apartment by the lakefront when I saw my brother. He was walking down the street with a very light jacket, looking as thin as a stick, wearing pants and a shirt that he may have worn for days. He was going up to people and telling them he was homeless – asking them for money. I wasn't certain if he was living at home, or maybe in a halfway house near where I lived.

But I didn't want Harry to see me, knowing that he'd want to spend time together and know where I lived. I also suddenly panicked that I might again confront the guilt I just went through. I couldn't avoid seeing him, driving next to where he was walking down the sidewalk. But instinctively, I pulled my head down, fading deeply into the seat of my car while driving, barely seeing out of the windshield for him not to notice me.

After passing him by, I quickly turned down a side street. I wanted to be certain he didn't see me in my car. When I no longer saw him, I went down another street to return to where I was going. I felt disgusted knowing he was begging from people, let alone near where I lived. I needed to forget what he'd become. I wanted no one to know he was my brother. I had to protect my life and didn't want to have anything to do with him.

I didn't have any regret not stopping to see my brother. The life I had was very different than his, and I couldn't jeopardize that. Any contact with him or my mother, I felt certain would ruin me. I had worked that hard to leave home the way I did and put what I had behind me to lead a normal life. I couldn't sacrifice myself now – not even for my brother.

But I couldn't forget that he'd been robbed of his future at the most pivotal time of life, being a young adult, when a person's legacy is just being formed. How often I dwelled on that, wondering if my mother knew what she did to him. But seeing her unconscionable trauma too often, without professional help after that much loss, and what she'd been through in the Holocaust, things couldn't have been much different.

I was fortunate, in that my brother's life wasn't mine, but every bit of the guilt I'd carried often overcame me. As I grew older, I had to live even more feeling the guilt that I betrayed him, let alone my mother when they needed me most. I just couldn't understand why I felt this way – knowing what staying with them probably would have done to me?

The past I grew up with also followed me into relationships with two girlfriends. Both of the women weren't Jewish and their names didn't sound like they were – Jill Mensen and Anna Tourin.

Neither of them developed long-term not due to each person themself, but how much my mother had forbidden her sons to intermarry. When I was a kid, she told me two things that never left me – "Only marry someone Jewish" and "You must promise when I die that you'll give me a traditional Jewish funeral." There were no compromises.

Despite all my growth after I left home, a committed relationship with a non-Jewish girl would never happen. I felt enough shame that often ate me up in synagogue, coming to services with Kathy and my father – let alone what I might have felt being in a relationship with someone who wasn't Jewish.

I didn't have any deep regrets that the relationship with Jill didn't last more than three to four months. It was pretty physical and I never felt that I loved her. She didn't believe in religion very much and might have been agnostic or even an atheist. There was no way she would have converted to Judaism. We just both really liked the sex for a while, until I realized that we were very different people.

Jill didn't tell me much about her past, but I could tell it followed her maybe even more than me. I almost felt that I was often judging her for being that angry of a person sometimes. I was pretty certain it was due to her past. But who was I to even think that way for not having far more understanding the way I was raised. I couldn't see that she was a victim, just like me. Jill must have not been able to help the way she reacted to what probably happened to her. The anger she let me see too often only let me feel she was flawed. But during the time we were together, I often didn't see the things in my past that also still impacted me.

Anna was different than Jill. The relationship was physical and someone I cared for, who cared for me even more. But after a few months, I didn't really see a future. She had strong Catholic views, and I knew she wouldn't have converted, even for me. I couldn't betray what my mother wanted, even not seeing her in five years.

As a little kid, I had been told probably far too often by a Holocaust survivor that was raised Orthodox to marry someone Jewish. How could that change? I don't think that I could have ever confronted the guilt – not only the betrayal of my mother, but also compromising some of my Jewish values. That was never more clear than when her family invited me for dinner to celebrate Easter.

It was the first time I ever celebrated that holiday, being Jewish. But I didn't mind, I enjoyed spending time with Anna's family until that day. It had been the best of both worlds – enjoying how much in the first couple months I wanted to be around her and her family. I couldn't get enough of Anna's tenderness, knowing how much she cared about me – cooking for me at least a few times a week, helping to clean my apartment – and she was real attractive.

She had thick, wavy, medium brown hair, deep brown eyes that underlined the glow in her face and a thin, distinct, well-proportioned body. We both also liked Italian food, especially her Pasta Fagiolo that she cooked a few times a week for me. Italian cuisine was her specialty, learning from her mother how to prepare many dishes, being raised in a big Italian family.

The main entrée for Easter dinner was ham, which I didn't eat. Ham was not Kosher. It wasn't that I was Kosher, but I was raised Orthodox up to my Bar Mitzvah. That and any pork I just never really ate, let alone not being eaten in many Jewish homes. But after my brother's nervous breakdown, a month before my Bar Mitzvah, our family was no longer the same. We didn't continue remaining Orthodox.

Easter dessert became a reenactment of my mother's stories of the Holocaust. Firstly, there were chocolate and raspberry sparkled cookies in the shape of Easter bunnies that I also couldn't eat. But what triggered me was a 14-inch chocolate cake with white icing that was designed with a thick blue crucifix and Jesus Christ nailed to the cross. It covered the entire top of the cake.

I just couldn't stop staring at the cross. How could I not? I'd never even been in a church and couldn't the way I was raised. A crucifix was foreign to me. My face felt like it dropped to the floor, being in shock when I knew that people would eat the cake. I didn't know how anyone could – Jews or non-Jews.

Anna's mom cut a few slices of the cake and asked me if I wanted a piece. I said no, excused myself and ran to the bathroom, being nauseous and having a panic attack. I was boiling over with anxiety, feeling like I was breathing in unbearable heat.

The cross didn't only resemble non-Jewish religion, but in my eyes it was a Nazi swastika. I was terrorized, reminded of my mother's stories of the gas chambers, crematoriums, the two lines in Auschwitz for who lived and died, how her family was murdered and the life she lived in the camps. That darkness penetrated so deeply inside me that sometimes I thought that any symbols of religion that weren't Jewish reminded me of Nazis and what they did to my mother and her family.

The laws for Orthodox and Conservative observance in the Jewish religion will not let you intermarry. I knew with Anna not only couldn't I marry her, but as the relationship developed, it began to feel that I'd abandoned my religious and moral values. I was doing what my father did – being with a Shiksa, despite how I was raised. Especially after Easter dinner, sometimes I couldn't move past feeling that much betrayal of my mother, when I was with her. After that night, when ever I remembered the cross on the Easter cake, it sometimes even left me feeling that Anna and her family were Nazis.

One night being with her after Easter, I had been triggered by mother's trauma that had never left me and heard her unrelenting words of condemnation for Kathy burning in my mind.

> "She is a German and her family were Nazis. You must never forget what I'm telling you. We can never trust her and you can't have anything to do with her. We have to stay far away from the Deichke. I don't know what I will do to you, if you ever talk to her."

"Harry and I would rather that she be dead, knowing how much I suffered, and that my family was murdered in Auschwitz and Belzec. Her family may even be responsible. I know some of them were Nazis who murdered every Jew they could find."

I wished I could have looked at Anna differently and not let religion matter. But my feelings towards her couldn't overcome how I was raised and what I promised my mother. I wanted to but couldn't be like my father. She cared about me often it seemed unconditionally, which made me feel only closer to her. But growing up in an Orthodox home and with the mother I had, if only to live without the guilt, I couldn't be with someone that wasn't Jewish.

But my father did what always made him happy, even if he had to pay for it – knowing what my mother did to us to hate him as much as we did, let alone our feelings about Kathy. As I'd told, I don't know how he even assimilated her into Chicago's Jewish community and the neighborhood where they lived. When he began living with her in the early 1960's, I'd mentioned there were many Jewish people in Chicago, including some of their friends who were Holocaust survivors.

It was less than 20 years after the Holocaust. He never looked at my stepmother differently, even though she wasn't Jewish. But that couldn't have been me the way I was raised. The unforgettable irony was that a Nazi saved my mother and over 1200 other Jewish lives. Without my German stepmother, I felt that I probably wouldn't have lived.

After the relationships with Anna and Jill, I left Motorola near my mid 20's. I worked in a few different positions for a couple years. I couldn't find the right job and bounced around between companies. There was finally a position with a giftware company – Silvestri – in finance that I stayed in for a while.

I don't know the reason exactly, but maybe just some more time in a normal life without my mother also began to change some of the hatred I felt for my Kathy.

When I could start letting go of some of the control my mother still had over me, I began to see her a little differently. I finally had realized she played a role in helping me get to where I was now. While my feelings began to change, they still weren't even close to what I needed them to be. What began as a child that I was trying to escape also would unforgettably impact me by what happened next.

CHAPTER VI

Her Diagnosis

After Scott and I had lived together for a couple years, I moved out of our place by the lake to Glenview. It's a northern suburb of Chicago. He had a girlfriend and I was dating a few people, but we just both needed our space. It got to a point where there were some bad arguments between us when either of us had someone over. Both of us thought the other person shouldn't have a girl over when the other was home. We even fought about it a few times, but it never resolved anything.

When I told him I was moving out, it seemed he was upset, since we had a lease and he'd now be paying my half of the rent. Scott also thought I owed him some of the security deposit when I left because the lease wouldn't end for another four months. I didn't agree with him, since he was keeping the apartment. But honestly, he could have been right. I wanted to leave that badly, but couldn't afford the new deposit, while paying him half the old one for our place. When I left, we talked again after a few months passed, but it was never the same. He really thought I screwed him.

I couldn't have been happier, moving out of my place with Mitch. I loved my privacy and for the first time in my life I paid for everything and wasn't dependent on anyone anymore. I wasn't obligated to my dad, or a roommate – no one told me what to do. The guilt that also followed me when I left home no longer seemed like it did anymore. I was no longer manipulated by my past, at least temporarily, not being dependent on anyone.

I had lived in my apartment for six months when one late December Saturday afternoon my stepmother called me. I had just returned home from the gym feeling like I was "walking on water" after a very intense workout. I was also excited thinking about my 25th birthday only a few months away – feeling being older and more independent would let my stepmother and father see me as a far more respected adult than before.

When Kathy called, she told me that she had seen my mother walking on Devon Avenue in West Rogers Park. She asked me whether my mother had suddenly lost a lot of weight, since she looked deathly thin and convinced she was sick. I told Kathy that I hadn't seen her in maybe three years and she was heavy the last time I remembered.

I asked her if she was certain the woman that saw was actually my mother. She waited a second before answering and then angrily told me, "Don't you think I know what your mother looks like?" I didn't reply, knowing it wasn't worth arguing with her. Otherwise, she'd become even more angry – insulting me with no regret. You could never change her mind when she had that tone in her voice.

After we talked for a few minutes, Kathy demanded that I take my mother to see a doctor on Monday morning. I couldn't get what she told me about my mother out of my mind, even for a moment. What she said also reminded me of every bit of guilt that I confronted when I left home – too often feeling I abandoned her as I became older.

> "This is your mother. You're her son and it's your duty. I know you haven't talked to her in years. But if you don't take her, no one else will."

I replied:

> "I haven't seen her for over a half a decade and I can't forget why I left home. She may not even let me take her to the doctor. You think she trusts me? I wouldn't."

Kathy said.

> "I know what she did to you and me, but she still needs someone and you know there's nothing left of your brother. This is something you have to do."

I replied by saying.

> "I'll take her. I don't know if they'll let me take off from work. We're very busy. But I'll tell them it's an emergency – my mother is that sick."

It was shocking to know that Kathy even cared about what happened to my mother. I don't know if I could have, if I was her. How much hatred there was between them. They had no feelings for each other.

I was pretty selfish after I first replied to her, realizing my mother had to be very sick by what she told me. It just wasn't normal for her to suddenly lose a considerable amount of weight. But as cold as it sounds after what I'd heard, I didn't want to be bothered with her at the time. My life was going well, and I didn't want to be reminded anymore of the guilt that I felt again, knowing I'd have to see her. It didn't even matter knowing everything else she'd gone through. I was a victim the way I grew up, and I had to protect myself.

I guess what changed my mind was actually guilt – knowing how much how often that I'd felt I abandoned my mother. I'd said that I left home anyways, despite knowing her holocaust trauma was spiraling and she'd be living with my brother. He often wasn't too mentally stable, even after he left a psychiatric hospital or halfway house. There was also the shame of not having seen my mother for that long until knowing she was probably that sick.

When I hung up the phone with Kathy, I didn't consider what I would say to my mother when I picked her up in the next couple days. Maybe she wouldn't even come with me. How would I also confront my guilt, feeling that I left her when she probably needed me that much?

What I didn't want to feel more of, especially now might even seem more real. Would I question whether leaving home, even if for my own survival was justified? I didn't know how hard it might be to overcome the promise to my mother growing up. I was certain that when I called her, I'd remind myself how I always needed to be there for her. I called my mother 15 minutes after I talked to Kathy to tell her I wanted to take her to the doctor Monday morning.

> "Mom I know that I haven't talked to you in a while, but are you sick? I saw you the other day on Devon Avenue, I had to get back for a work deadline so I didn't stop, but you looked much too thin."

> "Why have you suddenly lost a ton of weight? What's wrong? I have to take you to a doctor. It can't wait. I'll pick you up Monday morning."

She answered and said:

> "Bobby, my shana yiengele. Why did you leave me? Wasn't
> I a good mother to you? I protected you, but you left me
> to be with a Shiksa. How could you do that to me? You
> know how I raised you?"

> "I didn't lose weight. What are you talking about? You
> haven't seen me in that long. How would you know if I
> looked different after all these years?"

I didn't answer her questions. I knew that if I did I might feel all the guilt again of how I left her and my brother in their condition. But I wouldn't stop demanding that I take my mother to a doctor and telling her it was an emergency. Finally, I couldn't control myself anymore and yelled at her for not listening to me.

> "How can you do this to yourself? What if you're really sick?
> Don't you want to live for a while? You don't need to suffer
> the way you have all these years."

> "You've only trusted health foods and natural medicines
> when you're sick. But they never worked much. If you don't
> go with me on Monday, I won't see you again. I mean it."

She finally agreed to let me pick her up Monday morning. I didn't want to mention that Kathy was the one who had recently seen her and told me that she must be pretty sick. I felt she only would have thought it was my betrayal of her, if she knew that I even talked to my stepmother. She never would have agreed to let me take her to the doctor. My mother always felt I'd betrayed her whenever I mentioned that I'd talked to Kathy.

I didn't want to answer my mother when she questioned why I left home or told me that she didn't lose any weight. There was already enough guilt when I first heard her voice, let alone reacting to when she asked me why I left home, replaced her with my stepmother and had not seen her what she felt was ages. I also wouldn't answer when she questioned my observations of her health. I knew she wouldn't liked what I'd tell her.

My mother never took care of herself, didn't see doctors, ate spoiled food, was overweight for years, smoked for a while, and went to hospitals only if there was an emergency. She only had medical insurance for a major illness that didn't cover certain things and felt doctors and hospitals charged too much. Despite not working, she could have paid for better insurance. We lived in a nice suburb and she saved every dime my father gave her for alimony and child support.

She often preferred natural methods rather than going to the doctor for medical care. I knew that was due to her survivor trauma after the Holocaust. Thank God, somehow her trauma had never prevented me and my brother from being seen by a doctor. I remember her going to a health food store in Chicago on Devon Avenue for natural remedies to treat everything from a cold and stomach flu to an ear infection. She once even went to a hypnotist when she couldn't get rid of cramps due to her period.

A lot of survivors didn't trust doctors after the Holocaust. How could they, knowing German doctors tortured and murdered Jews in the concentration camps? Most traumatic for them, I expect, was the "Selection Process" of who lived and died in the death camps, not to mention the Nazis' deranged experiments on prisoners. These included "high altitude" experiments in which camp inmates were forced without oxygen into high altitude chambers that replicated conditions of up to 68,000 feet, as well as the removal of human bones, nerves and muscle from prisoners. That even included amputation of their whole legs that were transplanted to other victims.

After one of the longest weekends in my life, wondering what I would say to my mother or feel when I saw her, not seeing her for nearly seven years, I picked her up at 7:30 Monday morning. The doctor's appointment wasn't until 9:00 and his office was only 40 minutes away, but I wanted plenty of time before we left. I didn't know what to expect.

I came in the house from the back entrance and saw her sitting in a chair near the end of the dining room. I wanted to be more discreet than coming in the front door – already being too nervous about my feelings when I saw her. The house hadn't changed much since I left. I couldn't believe that I had lived in such disgusting filth. Nothing was different, and I couldn't wait to leave. I hadn't lived that way in many years. When I first came in in the back way, I walked into the kitchen and there was spoiled food in the refrigerator, the bathtub and toilet in the guest bathroom downstairs hadn't been cleaned and the carpets were deeply stained.

I finally moved nearer to where my mother was sitting in the dining room. She wouldn't stop looking at me. But I only glanced at her for a moment, while she wouldn't take her eyes off of me. If I looked at her more, I feared it could trigger compassion for her that I no longer had felt. But as I moved closer to see her better, even unwillingly, I had to look at her directly.

"How are you?"

She only said:

"Let me get my coat and purse."

Even when she went to get them, she just kept staring at me with a smile. I could tell that she didn't want me to leave. When I looked at her face, it was nearly in tears. She looked over at me and then asked me a question I knew was coming.

"Are you moving home?"

"I have a home," I said.

I didn't say anything more to her, except that we had to leave. "Let's go, otherwise we'll miss the doctor's appointment."

She was every bit as thin as Kathy told me and didn't look my mother anymore. She was always on the heavier side, except when I was a little kid. The guilt of leaving her and seeing her like this, not having seen her for that long was eating me up inside.

Every time I thought of her after I left home, I couldn't let myself feel more than I wanted to. As I've told, I felt the feelings could ruin me. But I couldn't protect myself any longer from my emotions, especially the guilt – knowing that she could even be dying. Still, compassion for others should be a desire to want to help them, not that we're forced to feel that way. The costs of compassion for someone when it's driven by guilt are the resentment and even bitterness may stay with you for a lifetime.

Once we were driving to the doctor's, my mother began to stare at me at again. Her eyes were fixated on me, and I'm pretty certain she didn't look anywhere else. Finally she asked me a question, and said a few other words. She needed to tell me that she missed me more than ever and to move back home. She couldn't be alone.

"I hope you're eating well. Do you miss me? I wish you'd come back home. You know how much I miss you. I need you to move back here."

Silence filled the car. These were things that I didn't want to hear. I had to be stronger than I'd ever been not to say anything. Any conversation might trigger feelings of responsibility – that I needed to to take care of her, especially after everything that she'd gone through. In the past I didn't have to confront what I couldn't. I was able to hide when she came over to my apartment in Wheeling, and the time she called me when I lived with Scott. But this was different. There was nowhere to go. I was driving her to the doctor's and afraid of being alone with her in the car.

What if had to confront my guilt? It might have led to wanting to reconcile our relationship. Instead, we didn't talk the rest of the way to the doctor's. I didn't want to confront anything I might begin to feel for her again. I'd help her, but only from a distance. It's what I had to do. I couldn't return to what I left.

My mother needed compassion, but I couldn't give her enough of what she needed. I couldn't forget that what she did to me and my brother often felt inhuman. Still, her actions were defenses to what she went through. How many people would have acted much differently, if they had gone through what she did? But I couldn't put aside my resentment of her, even now.

I wished that I could have found some of the way Schindler opened up his heart. He finally put aside his obsession with money and the exploitation of Jews, which let him fulfill his ambitions. What mattered to him had been transformed for my mother and the more than 1200 other Jewish lives he saved. He finally stood apart from how the Nazis and so many others looked at Jews. Someone that found compassion for the innocent after seeing the unconscionable dehumanization of their lives during the Holocaust.

When we arrived at the doctor's office, my mother asked me why she had to see someone, since she didn't feel sick. I was relentless just like when I called her and finally said that I wouldn't see her again, if she didn't see a doctor.

> "You've lost far more weight than what's normal for a woman of your size. I'm really worried that you're pretty sick. There must be something wrong with you and we need to find out what it is."

She first answered and said:

> "Does it matter? Harry's sick and he won't get better. I
> don't ever see you. There's no one who cares about me.
> I'm just alone."

But even despite what she said, she reconsidered and decided to let the doctor examine her. There was nothing I could have done if she didn't want to be helped, but I had to believe this wasn't how it would end. How could she just give up? She didn't being only a little older than her 16th birthday, when her family began to be murdered in the gas chambers and what the Nazis might have been doing to her. She survived with hope that never died, despite what life must have been like – being alone in the Krakow Ghetto, deported to Plaszow and Auschwitz.

If not for her will to live, Oskar Schindler never would have been able to save her. Maybe that was what she thought of when she agreed to let the doctor finally examine her. In that moment, I wished she would have told me about Schindler and what he did. It might have let me move past what I went through and to be learning for the rest of my life – that you never give up hope, especially the will to live, no matter what you're confronting. Our conviction to those values can change what you didn't feel was possible.

The doctor gave my mother a complete physical, but I wasn't in the exam room. But he would let me know his findings and whether further tests would be required. I waited for an hour, becoming increasingly impatient. That one hour felt like several. I was very nervous that she was that sick. The weight she'd lost was shocking after being heavy nearly my whole life. In not seeing doctors, eating spoiled food and her face and body being a fraction of what they were, there had to be something really wrong with her.

After he finished examining her, he walked into the room, came to where I was sitting and told me, "Your mother has to see an oncologist. She may have cancer from the blood tests I've completed." He told me if that's what it is, she may have colon or pancreatic cancer. But he wasn't certain. Finally, he said "when someone who has a sudden and severe loss of weight, they're common symptoms for gastrointestinal cancer."

When he weighed her, she was only 85 lbs. But the normal weight for a woman her height was 105 lbs. After hearing what the doctor said, I was pretty certain she had cancer. When I lived at home she always weighed between 135 – 140. Even the few times I saw her momentarily over the years, she was always pretty heavy.

At first, I wasn't in shock or stunned by the news. As I'd felt I knew there was something was wrong with her. She had probably lost 45 lbs in the past two to three months. The doctor also said he told my mother after he examined her that she may have cancer. But even knowing she was probably very sick, I had some denial. Wouldn't anybody at first, if they knew a family member, let alone their mother might be diagnosed with cancer.

But after a little while longer, hearing what the doctor said, it was real and the news began to really hit me. I slumped deep into my chair in the waiting room. Then some tears began to rush down over my face. I realized that my mother could very well have cancer. How would I even begin to discuss this with her? I was only 25 and had never been responsible for anyone, let alone my mother. How could I ask for my father's help? I certainly couldn't from Kathy – knowing how they also felt about each other. Even after my brother's nervous breakdown, I never had to take care of him. My parents knew it was their responsibility.

She came out of the waiting room, and sat down next to me. I turned to her.

"Do you know what the doctor told you?"

"Yes," she said.

I didn't ask anything further. How could I listen to how she felt knowing that she may have cancer? If I heard what that meant to her, how could I not fall apart? When we drove to the doctor's, I couldn't even talk to her, despite knowing how much she missed me and wanted me to come home. I couldn't let myself break down when she may need me most. How would that help her, if I was a mess? I told her we'd call the oncologist and see if we could get an appointment in the next week. I also said, if it turns out to be cancer, there's treatment or surgery available, especially if it's not too advanced.

When we drove home, she really didn't say much to me, and I didn't know what to say to her. I was doing what was necessary to find out what was wrong with her and determine what needed to be done. But I couldn't give any more of myself, particularly the love that maybe I should have let her feel. I might have been selfish, but I looked at it being purely for my own self preservation. I just felt there was too much that I'd done after I left home to get where I was with my life.

After I parked the car when we came to the house, I walked my mother to the door. I told her that I would let her know when I had the appointment with the oncologist and what time I'd pick her up. We just looked at each other for a few minutes before she went inside. I thought she would tell me again how much she missed me and needed me to be with her, but she didn't.

Maybe she was preoccupied, feeling that her future wasn't long and reflecting upon the past – why I left, what happened to my brother, or why she was alone. I didn't know what to say to her. I was overcome by so much pity for her tragic life. Everything that she had gone through since she was just 16 and what she might face now. She wasn't even that old – recently turning 62. I was pretty certain if we did talk, there would be a breaking point where I felt she couldn't be alone, and I would move back home. But as I'd said, I just couldn't give up what I had.

When I left my mother's, I went home and called Kathy. I told her the doctor said that she may have cancer. I also said if it was, that it might be colon or pancreatic cancer due to her sudden loss of weight. Finally, I mentioned that I called an oncologist the doctor recommended and he'd have to do some additional tests. She didn't have much to say after what I told her, except repeated the same word more than a few times.

"Ahuh, Ahuh, Ahuh," she said.

I assumed Kathy was processing what I told her. Sometimes she replied that way at first when there was news she didn't want to hear. I also felt she probably wouldn't let herself give my mother the compassion I might have expected by what she could have to confront. Her feelings about my mother probably ran way too deep. The only other thing she said to me was that I had to take her to the oncologist and the hospital for any tests.

"It's your responsibility to take her wherever she has to go. She's your mother."

I replied and said:

"Yes, I will, but I'm not certain if she'll need any tests in the hospital. I'll know more after we see the doctor.

"I'll probably have to ask for a little time off work and tell them that I recently learned my mother is pretty sick. I have to let them know she may have cancer and there's no one else to take her to doctor's appointments."

I thought my stepmother would have been more involved with my mother's care after learning that she might have cancer. She knew that I never had to face anything like this before. But when Kathy barely expressed any feelings by what I told her, I was certain that she wouldn't help. But I had to, there was no one else. Otherwise, if she was too sick and couldn't do anything for herself or wasn't willing, she might die. I couldn't live with that guilt.

I picked up my mother to see the oncologist a few weeks after she'd be seen by her internist. We didn't say much to each other in the car. She asked me how I was doing, and I asked her. It was just a few passing words, but nothing meaningful. I had to remain functional and couldn't say more to her, but I would have liked to know what she was thinking.

If I had put myself in her position for what she might have been going through, I just couldn't not have reacted to maybe having cancer. But I was far younger than she was and developing the way I did after I left home, I couldn't have been more filled with hope for a real future ahead of me. There was that much for me to live for now. She never had much from her life, even after everything she went through in the Holocaust. Her thoughts might have only been far more accepting than I would have – probably feeling that her illness was no longer only possible but becoming real.

The doctor I brought her to see had taken a little while to find. My mother wanted a Jewish doctor, preferably Orthodox, given how she was raised. After learning what German doctors did to Jews in the Holocaust, even maybe to herself, how could she trust anyone else? I called a few of her old friends and one of them recommended someone to me. His name was Dr. Lipschutz. He wasn't Orthodox, but it was the best I could do on such short notice.

We arrived at Dr. Lipschutz's office a little early for her 11:30 appointment. It didn't start on time because he and one of his colleagues wanted to review the blood tests that were done by her internist. He specialized in treating cancer and would be more certain of the results than the other doctor.

The nurse finally called my mother into the doctor's office. I went with her, because I didn't want her to hear what the doctor would say alone. If it was cancer, I'd have to know what to do next. He looked at my mother for a few seconds and then began to feel her abdomen and her lower back. He asked her if it hurt where he was pressing. She said it did a little bit. He then asked her to sit up on the exam table, while I sat in a chair next to her.

I didn't want to hear what Doctor Lipschultz would say, but I'm not certain if my mother did or didn't. Suddenly, the guilt that I felt for abandoning her when I left home just wouldn't stop replaying in my head. It was also shocking, looking at her being silent – not even emotional.

> "Mrs. Don, the blood tests we've done confirm that you have colon cancer. It might be more advanced than we thought, due to your sudden loss of so much weight in the last two months."

> "I'd like to do an exploratory surgery within the next week. We'll remove the tumor(s) we find and biopsy them. We may be able to do chemotherapy first or remove any other tumors that are found and then give you chemotherapy."

> "It depends what stage the cancer is in currently. The second option is best for preventing the cancer from spreading or returning. I'm very sorry Mrs. Don."

After what he'd said, neither of us asked him many questions. It was what I felt that I knew, only by seeing how thin she was. But I still wasn't ready to hear what he told us. I felt my mother also knew by her silence. She probably even felt some acceptance, when her doctor – internist first told her that she might have cancer. After the life she had, there might have been a part of her that just wanted it to end.

The only question I really asked him was if he would set up the arrangements for the surgery. He said that he would and scheduled the procedure for the exploratory procedure and biopsy next Thursday. He wanted it done at Michael Reese, which was in Chicago. He was on staff with the hospital. I didn't want to be bothered finding another doctor for a second opinion. I trusted what he told us.

When we left the doctor's office, I drove my mother home, and we didn't say much to each other. After hearing what the doctor said, I didn't care anymore about protecting myself from being reminded of my guilt. My mother had cancer and I needed to know what she was feeling. I knew I owed that to her. Regardless of why I left home, she brought me into this world, and I needed to find a way to care more about her feelings. I finally asked if she would please tell me whatever she needed to say.

"What am I supposed to tell you?" she answered. "I never had that much from my life except you kids. You and Harry, at least for a while."

"Your father took what was left of me when he married his Shiksa. I wish he knew how much I loved him, before he left me."

"I just hope you don't leave me now. I don't have anyone else. You know there is nothing Harry can do for me."

After thinking about what she just told me, nothing else mattered. I was in tears hearing what she said. It let me begin a little to see the world through her eyes more than I had been. After I'd left home, I never wanted to do that again. But I'd mentioned sometimes that didn't happen when I confronted the guilt for leaving her. As I grew older, I've probably said more than enough that I felt my brother and I were victims and she was responsible. Still better understanding what she'd gone through over time, I've repeatedly had to question how could things really have been different. I'd said she was filled with trauma, living with the intense emotional pain of what happened to her in the Holocaust without psychological help, that her sons inherited. It came from a life no one would have wanted to live. Finally, I said a few things to my mother that I never could.

"Mom, I wish that I knew what to tell you. I know what you went through, which probably no one who did would understand. All I know is you raised me since I was a little kid to believe in God and the Jewish religion."

"I've always felt that I what learned being raised Jewish, knowing what happened to Jews throughout history, is that the Torah tells us to never give up hope and the future can be better. There's no other way you survived the Holocaust."

"I will do what I can to be there for you. You know I have a job and my own place. I can't give that up, move back home and stay with you. But you're right. There's no one else to help you. I'll remember that."

My mother didn't say anything else to me, which I didn't expect, especially after I told her that I couldn't move back home. Maybe she knew that I'd grown up and overcome some of the guilt, despite the way she raised me. I hadn't seen her for a long time and hadn't said much to her, even knowing how sick she probably was. She must have known that my feelings towards her had changed after I left home.

I had said what I wanted to say, but still felt that I could only be there for her from a distance. She would have wanted me to be with her every second and I couldn't do that. I wanted to help her, but I couldn't sacrifice myself, even for her illness. If I moved back home, I also would have seen my brother sometimes – if he wasn't hospitalized or in a halfway house.

I couldn't forget why I left – wanting to get as far away as I could from her spiraling trauma. I didn't want to tell her that no matter what she had gone through it didn't give her the right to do what she did to me, and especially my brother. If I had said something to her, it might have triggered my guilt feeling I abandoned her when I left home. How could I tell her what she did to us, despite that maybe it couldn't have been helped, knowing she might be dying?

It was a blessing my mother knew her surgery was being done at Michael Reese. The hospital was founded by a Jewish immigrant in the 1880's, and carried on a long commitment to serve Chicago's Jewish community. I would have preferred a hospital closer and not in the inner city, but there probably wouldn't have been one with a deep history tied to the Jewish community. How could I not honor her wishes, knowing she needed every bit of comfort for what she needed to and might face.

The irony of her need for Jewish practitioners was that Oskar Schindler, the person that saved her life, wasn't only not Jewish, but a Nazi German. He was part of a race and nation that couldn't be trusted, except for him. Kathy's family also were people that could be trusted, despite what my mother felt. Her father died not giving up that trust in front of his family. These things needed to be told to me and my brother growing up, and yet they never were. We paid the price for not knowing. And I'll never be able to say enough it couldn't have been more fatal than for my brother.

It was finally Thursday morning, and I picked up my mother and drove her to the hospital. It was a bitterly cold day in late January. When I was driving to her house, I was that scared; what if I actually learned there was nothing that could be done for her? The palms of my hands were sweating from anxiety. It made the steering wheel too hard to hold at times, being that slippery.

I watched cars on the road passing me by, yet my mind was somewhere else. If the doctors found out after surgery her cancer couldn't be treated, how would I ever reconcile my feelings of guilt? I couldn't forget that I left home when she was facing a crisis and hadn't seen her again for longer than I felt I ever could.

Once I picked her up and we drove to the hospital, we really didn't say much to each other. When I began seeing her again, we often didn't say much to each other. I didn't even know what to say most of the time. I've said that was also due to being too afraid it might trigger every bit of my guilt that I left her when she really needed me.

She probably also didn't want to talk much, probably being knowing how sick she could be, other than telling me to move back home. I knew my mother and was pretty certain that she wanted to forget what might be happening to her and go back to how life was when I was growing up. The little boy she'd protected too much. Someone who always needed his mother and only felt better when she was around.

After not saying anything to each other for a while as we were driving, there was one question she asked me.

"Will I be all right?

"I really hope so," I said to her calmly.

"Let's just get you to the hospital to find out how they can treat you, depending on how far the cancer has advanced."

"We need you to get well. I want you to have a fast recovery and a normal life. In the Jewish religion, you've always told me 'God tells us that we can never give up and the future can be better."

I continuously paced the floor of the busy waiting room after the surgery began. Dr. Lipschultz told me the surgery might last three hours. I was alone in the waiting room without Kathy or my father – uncontrollably nervous, impatient and feeling guilty that if I hadn't left home, this never would have happened. Neither my father or Kathy would have came me with to the hospital. I couldn't have expected them to, knowing the feelings between my mother and them.

But I wished Kathy would have been there with me. Despite all the years of bitterness towards my mother, her compassion for me might soften the guilt I was confronting. It might help me again realize how much I needed to leave home for my survival. Maybe she'd even feel some sympathy for her because of me. While I was pretty certain my father wouldn't have consoled me very much if he'd came. He wouldn't have been nearly as compassionate as Kathy. I knew how much he hated my mother.

I looked at the clock maybe three or four times in the waiting room, anxiously wondering if I could wait that long to hear the news of her fate. If the surgeons came out much earlier, I didn't think it was a good sign. I felt it meant there was nothing they could do for her. Finally, right before 1:00 Dr. Lipschultz and another doctor who assisted with my mom's surgery came to where I was waiting and led me to a far corner of the room to talk with me privately.

> "We discovered from the exploratory procedure that a larger tumor we biopsied has stage 4 colon cancer. Her diagnosis is terminal, and the cancer will continue to spread into other areas of her body."

> "She's only expected to live 3 to 4 months. If we had known earlier, maybe we could have done something. But there is nothing we can do anymore."

> "Your mother is in recovery and we haven't told her anything yet. We wanted to see if you wanted us to tell her ourselves, with you, or for you to only talk to her."

> "There's no one else that can tell her she's dying. I have to tell her myself."

The doctors told me they'd discharge her within the next day and give her a colostomy bag and catheter for bowel movements and urinating. They told me I'd need a nurse for her during the day to empty the colostomy bag and catheter that would be attached to her and monitor her pain. They made me aware that she'd get much weaker in the next three to four weeks, remaining in bed most of the day.

I was also told the colon cancer had spread into some other areas of her body. I'd have to get medication for her pain that would rapidly get worse. Her appetite would shrink and she'd begin to eat very little, while getting more sedentary and become even thinner. The doctors also mentioned that most cancer patients develop jaundice in their face and hands.

Finally they said that when my mother was a few weeks from dying that I should strongly consider hospice care. Dr. Lipschultz would give me some names of caregivers that his office recommended. The doctors said hospice lets patients who are terminally ill die with much more comfort and dignity than they would otherwise.

They had given me this shocking news with a deeply cold, unemotional sensitivity. After I heard the diagnosis, I ran to the men's bathroom, didn't say a word, clenched my hands, despite feeling barely conscious, took my right fist and punched the men's hand dryer with rage I'd never felt. I'd hit the dryer that hard it cracked in half.

Somehow, I regained my composure and went back to the waiting room. Fortunately no one saw what happened. While a man had entered the bathroom when I was leaving, he didn't pay any attention to the cracked hair dryer and it didn't seem that he heard anything.

After I went back to the waiting room, I had to know immediately what hospital bed my mother would be transferred to from surgery. The doctors said they wouldn't tell her she was dying, but I was scared that someone else would mistakenly say something to her. But she had to hear from that me and be told now. It couldn't wait, I owed her that. I'd want all the time that could be given to me and felt she needed that too, confronting dying too soon.

There was also so much else running through my mind. How could I help her, never having even known anyone that was dying, let alone my own mother? I was also overwhelmed by that if I saw her too much, I didn't know how I'd protect my life and everything I did to get where I was. But at the same time, I didn't want to not be with her enough knowing what she was going through. I just knew that I didn't know how I'd cope with the guilt that I'd been reminded of too often after I left home. It probably would never trigger me more than now – knowing that she was going to die in a few months.

My mother was in recovery for an hour after surgery before she was taken to her room. I was already waiting for her, panicking, not knowing what I would say to her. Sweat covered my forehead and stained my shirt below my underarms. I paced the floor of the small private room until I was nearly dizzy. I replayed in my mind and out loud what I would say to her, but I couldn't think straight. There was no way to prepare myself for telling her what no one would want to hear.

I looked at her when she returned, lying in a bed, wearing a hospital gown, her thin strands of hair that hadn't been washed in a few days, and her colostomy bag being attached to her. Her catheter was connected to tubes that were also attached to her.

My mother didn't say anything to me when she came to her room. She was probably in some pain and very tired due to the anesthesia. But she smiled when she saw me waiting for her. I didn't really smile back – knowing what I had to tell her in the next few minutes. Emotionally, I had to keep whatever distance I could from her, otherwise I would have broken down. I finally looked at her as best I could.

> "Mom, I don't know how to tell you this. The surgeons told me they saw a tumor in your colon that was large and didn't want to take it out being pretty certain of what I'll tell you next."

> "They biopsied a small part of the tumor. You have stage 4 colon cancer. It's in the most advanced stage and will continue to spread. There will be times when you're in pain, but you'll have good medication that will help, especially when you're feeling that bad."

> "Stage 4 cancer occurs before, before, before you da-da-da-die. They told me that you're only expected to live another three months. I couldn't have the doctors tell you. I had to be the one. I just wish it could be different."

When I said the words "before" and "die" to my mother, they wouldn't come out of my mouth fluently. I could only stutter when I said them to her. How was I supposed to say that to anyone, let alone my mother?

After she heard what I said, she didn't say much. What could she even say – lying in pain, barely awake and probably knowing that she was dying.?

> "Bobby, will you help me? I can't be alone and you know I have no one else. You know Harry is gornish (Yiddish word meaning "nothing"). I've been alone since you left, and I can't anymore, especially now."

I replied and said:

> "Mom, I will do all I can. I promise that I will come see you at least a few times a week. You'll have someone with you during the week and many weekends."

> "You have my phone number if you need anything. You know I can't move back home. It will be okay."

> "If needed, you'll also have someone with you at night. Let's see what happens."

After what I said, she didn't say anything, despite probably wanting far more from me. But she knew that too much time had passed since I left home. I no longer felt the attachment to her I couldn't live without growing up.

I had at least felt some relief after telling my mother what she needed to hear and setting a few boundaries. But it still didn't keep me from feeling I wasn't doing enough for her. This was my mother who raised me, despite what she did to me and my brother. Still, I couldn't resolve the guilt that I felt. She didn't have much from her life after what she went through and would die in only a few months. But despite everything that happened, I couldn't give her more. I still just couldn't sacrifice myself for her. Maybe that was selfish or just wise. Her fate was known, while mine was only beginning.

I drove her home the next day from the hospital and what could we really say to each other? We heard what the doctor said and nothing was going to change. What could I really tell her that would help what she might be going through? I think she'd just accepted what I told her.

But I listened to her continue to tell me that I needed to be with her. The words I'd heard repeatedly since I began to see her again. Though now, I couldn't be more certain that meant every second of the day. When she told me that, there were times that I could barely control myself after I knew she had cancer and might even be dying. I had to fight that hard not to have every bit of compassion for her. Otherwise what I felt might have taken me with her.

After driving her back home, we walked upstairs and I helped her change into a nightgown, placed a new sheet on the bed, propped up her pillows and covered with her a blanket.

I looked at her briefly and told her I was going. I said that I had to leave the house for a while, but I didn't tell her that I would call my stepmother. I needed to her tell her what the doctors had said and how much I needed her help now.

> "Mom, I'm getting your prescriptions from the pharmacy and maybe a few things from the grocery store for you – cheese, bread and I know you like goat milk. I'll be back in maybe an hour and a half."

I was glad my mother didn't really keep Kosher any more. It would make shopping for groceries that she'd need much easier. With Harry being sick and me no longer being home, keeping Kosher didn't matter much to her anymore. When we kept Kosher, it brought her the feeling of family and how she was raised before the Holocaust. But we no longer were a family.

After I left the house, I went to the pharmacy, purchased my mother's pain medications and then used a pay phone in the store to finally call my stepmother. I didn't want to call her right after the doctors told me my mother was going to die. I wasn't in the right place mentally to answer her questions. Though I was no longer in shock, I was overwhelmed by everything I was facing, knowing that a nurse and me would have to take care of everything for my mother – emptying her colostomy bag and catheter, cleaning the house, buying groceries and prescriptions, helping feed her, keeping her company, etc.

With a very serious tone in my voice, I began telling Kathy my mother's diagnosis.

> "My mother is very sick, she has stage 4 colon cancer and will not recover. The doctors feel she'll die in three to four months."

They told me that her cancer is in its final stage and there was nothing they could do.

> "I took her home from the hospital earlier today. After two months, she'll get very weak and suffer way more than she is now."

> "The pain will become nearly intolerable, until she can't leave her bed anymore. She'll also become less and less respondent."

"We'll have to hire a full-time nurse for managing her care. Once her pain gets worse, we'll have to give her morphine, that needs to be heavily increased when the pain is nearly intolerable."

"The doctors told me it's best that she enters hospice near the time before she dies. It's the last few weeks before she'll pass away."

"Honestly, I just don't know what to do. How will I take care of her with my job? I know you two hate each other and I was never really nice to you, but I can't do this alone."

"She made us believe that you took my father away from her, my brother and I. She told me that your family were Nazis and helped kill Jews in the concentration camps."

"But I know that your father couldn't stand what the Nazis were doing and died for what he believed in."

"There are things that I wish I could get past, growing up with the hatred I did, that I still have to confront. But, I just can't yet. Please understand, maybe someday that will change. Right now, she and I just need your help."

Kathy didn't say a word for a few minutes. Maybe she didn't know how to reply or how to even react. But she finally told me what she would do. It was barely more than a sentence.

"Ahuh, Ahuh, Ahuh," as she always reacted at first to news that was hard to hear.

"Meet me at your mother's house tomorrow and I'll see her for a little while."

I expected much more from her, telling her my mother was dying. While I knew everything that happened between them, she only had three or four months to live. I was also panicking when I told her that I didn't know what to do after what I heard. I needed her to calm me down, tell me that she'd be there for me, let alone my mother. I knew she wasn't a person who often expressed her emotions, but this time was different. Both of us were suffering that much.

I felt her not saying more than a few words was pretty cruel. It didn't seem that she had sympathy for what my mother was facing, or even myself. I guess nothing could come between their feelings for each other. But I didn't know how to accept that she couldn't have compassion for someone when they needed it most.

I knew Kathy would tell my father my mother was dying, but I didn't expect much help or empathy from him either. How could he bring himself to do anything for her – knowing only shortly after they were married, how much he began to hate her? He couldn't put aside his differences, even if it were to help me. As I've told, I was pretty certain he felt that she made him marry her against his will. But I also said, if there was someone else to blame far more, it was my grandmother.

We met at my mother's home by 5:00 PM the next day. It was only the day after discussing my mother's fate. I had never expected that Kathy and my mother would ever have a conversation, even when my mother was dying. They'd met only briefly once when I was 9 or 10. My father stopped by our house and my stepmother waited for him in the car. My mother rushed out of the house to get a better look at her. She was only a few feet away from his new red Mercedes and they stared at each other for a moment. But they never said a word to each other. They didn't need to, knowing how they felt about each other.

When we came in the house, Kathy walked through the first floor like someone who wanted to remodel the place, deciding what needed to be repaired and updated, and what furniture needed to be replaced. As I've told, it still looked like an old house and a dump, just like when I lived there. She then asked me a few questions when she was in the living room. What I heard from her felt like pretty harsh judgments.

> "How did you live here? This house is just really awful. It's like pigs lived here. Nay, Nay."

> "Everything is dirty and old – nothing is kept up, the lamps and some of the light switches don't work, the dining room table is cracked and the couch in the living room is badly torn."

> "Your mother never cared about how she lived with you kids. She only cared about not getting enough alimony from your father and telling you and Harry that he destroyed all of your lives, when he left her and married a Shiksa."

It wasn't surprising – even now for her to be that judgmental. But how could she say those things about my mother to me knowing she was dying? I always felt her being that critical and hardened was due to being overly disciplined by a strong-willed mother. She had grown up in wartime, despite being a German in the Holocaust. Her mother needed her to be more of an adult as a child. I'd said she also needed to raise Kathy that way, being the youngest of seven children without a father for most of her life.

I wish that I would have said something in my mother's defense in that moment. This wasn't the time to tell me how awful her house was, and what she didn't do for her children. As much as I owed Kathy for helping me leave home, I was overcome by guilt for not having come to my mother's defense.

We walked upstairs to my mother's bedroom and again my stepmother told me things that I didn't want to hear. How the carpeting was ruined, there were soiled rings around the bathtub, and scratches nearly everywhere over the sink in the bathroom. After the last thing she said and everything else I heard, it just gave me memories I needed to forget before I left home.

"Oh My God. You lived here. If only your father knew."

She always had to judge how she thought about me by often telling me how my father would have felt. I knew they often necessarily weren't his views, or he'd be as upset as she was. But she felt it helped her better validate her position when she was critical of things that I did.

We entered the bedroom and saw my mother looking thinner than even some pictures I remembered of Jews starving in the Holocaust. She was lying in bed wearing a white nightgown, her blanket uncovered, attached to a red colostomy bag and a tan catheter. Then she looked up and saw me and my stepmother.

Kathy was dressed as usual, wearing an elegant slacks outfit, coat, and carrying a Louis Vuitton purse with her well-styled blond hair and blue eyes. She leaned over to my mother in bed, but left more than enough room between them. I wasn't sure why she didn't want to come a little closer. But maybe she felt that she was contagious, being that sick. Or, I guess, she didn't want to get close to someone that hated her as much as my mother did.

"How are you, Rose?"

"Not so good," my mother said.

"I know you're not feeling well. I believe Bobby will get you a nurse and she'll help you you begin feeling better."

They weren't exactly the words I would have expected. I felt what she said was as short, cold and insensitive as when I panicked asking for her help with my mother, telling her that she was dying.

My stepmother wasn't a person of deep compassion by the way she was raised. But I just didn't want to accept that, knowing everything I was feeling about my mother. Still, she was someone who gave her heart through her actions. She helped me leave me home, when I had nowhere else to turn. It helped create a real future that otherwise could have led to my brother's crisis. How could she not feel as many would for my mother, if they were her. How easy is it to have genuine compassion for your enemies, despite someone that close to dying?

When my mother looked at Kathy, after we first entered her room, she didn't have much of a reaction, except she stared at her for a while. I didn't know if she didn't say anything due to being in that much pain or might have been in shock. But I could only imagine what my mother must have thought, seeing her darkest enemy in front of her after all these years, who she'd only seen once for a moment in the midst of darkness.

How that must have felt, the person she couldn't stand for a lifetime being there, let alone with her son, who she raised to feel about the Kathy way she did. At that moment, I couldn't even begin to realize how she might have been feeling - knowing that my father left her being pregnant with me for Kathy, a German women in 1961, less than 20 years after what she went through in the Holocaust. As I've told, that happened living in a Jewish community, let alone that most of my mother's friends were Holocaust survivors, and probably every other Jewish kid I knew had one or both of their parents who were survivors.

There also must have been unforgettable heartbreak, feeling how much I betrayed her, suddenly being there with my stepmother. I hadn't seen her for seven years and Kathy was dressed like someone out of a magazine, while we came to see her at the most dire time of her life. But maybe there was something that I'd remember could come from them seeing each other after all these years, something no one would have expected. I just didn't know how their lifetime of contempt for each other could be put aside, even now. The feelings between them would probably only end the way they began.

We left my mother's bedroom, closed the door and Kathy wanted us to talk downstairs. She didn't want my mother to hear anything when we said. But I wasn't certain why.

"Have you called a nurse?

I answered and said: "Yes, I've called a few places and I'm planning to call a few more later today. But I need your help."

Kathy replied by saying:

> "Let me also call a few places later today. I know that I'm more experienced than you at finding a nurse. I helped a friend who was pretty sick and hired some very good caretakers when my sister's husband in Berlin was dying."

> "We have to go grocery shopping for your mother and get her some real food. I'm pretty certain the food in the house isn't even fresh from what your father's told me."

After telling me that she'd actually be helping me with my mother, I couldn't stop feeling that I might have been wrong about who I felt she was. Maybe I let everything they'd been through weigh too heavily on what we can do for others who can't help themselves. Could I see that "what brings us together can overcome what pulls us apart?" There was hope that her seeing my mother lying there – knowing she was dying – might be enough to put aside at least some of what she felt.

After going downstairs, we both went into the kitchen. Kathy opened the top lid of the oven that was covered by long burn marks and dark food stains under the stove burners. There was a dark film of grease and thick food stains that covered the oven racks and the bottom of the oven. She was disgusted by what she'd seen. I knew she would judge my mother again or how she could live in this filth.

> "How could you have never come over here to help clean your mother's house? You needed to show her everything that I taught you the past seven years."

> "Why couldn't you have done that for her once you knew how to take care of your place? You must have realized that you lived in filth and that hasn't changed from what I've seen here today."

I replied and said:

> "You know I haven't seen my mother since I left home. I told you that I couldn't see her again and you know why I left. I also couldn't see Harry anymore. I just couldn't."

She responded by saying:

> "Bobby, I know, I know, but you're her son, if you didn't help her, who would? Harry can't even take care himself. She has no one else."

I didn't say anything more after what she told me, not wanting to argue. What if my mother overheard we were fighting? I didn't want to feel any guiltier than I often did in the past few months.

> "I will call you tomorrow night after I contact some of the nursing agencies," Kathy said. "Your mother needs someone as soon as possible. She really had nothing from her life. But it could have been different."

Once I drove home, I couldn't stop thinking about Kathy visiting my mother, despite that they'd never really seen each other before. She had been visited by her deepest enemy since the Holocaust. I could only wonder how her life could have been different, if they would have reconciled. Maybe they would never have been good friends, but at least she might have been amenable to some of the things that Kathy gave me and could have given her.

 How her life might have been different, if she'd learned a few things from my stepmother – taking care of her herself, how she looked and not living in a house with filth. But mostly, she might have resolved some of the hatred that had ruined her. I know it was triggered by an inconceivable past. But there might been hope for learning from what she had went through instead of reacting to what was done to her.

If only my mother could have known what reconciliation between them would have meant for her children. Harry might have turned out differently, instead of being overcome by the penetration of her hatred left in him for a women that wasn't deserved. I may have been able to have the relationship with my mother and even Kathy I never had and salvage some of what I'd lost growing up.

I was told by her that one of the Jewish religion's most sacred values is "not to hate others." But why did we have to hate other people based only upon my mother's perceptions – just assumptions without even any traces of the facts? That to me lies at the heart of racism we see in the world.

CHAPTER VII

The Next Three Months

I went to see my mother for a second time that week after seeing her with Kathy. When I came over, I looked around the living room and I almost couldn't stay –the carpets being covered with stains, cracks that ran throughout the floors and the thick coat of soiled dirt which lined the kitchen countertop.

I couldn't even check the refrigerator after seeing all the spoiled food in there the first time I came to my mother's house again. It was disgusting. How did I live that way for 18 years. Still, I was reminded of my guilt for having left home, as if I was betraying my mother even thinking about the house that way, knowing she was dying.

I went upstairs to my mother's bedroom after I'd seen how the house was a wreck downstairs. I asked her how she was feeling. She said that she was in some pain, but needed me to take her to the washroom. That wouldn't be easy, since she couldn't walk much, and I'd almost have to carry her. She wanted me to wash her face a little bit since she was sweaty from lying in bed since last night. I also had to empty out her colostomy bag that was full. It smelled just as nauseating as you'd expect. After I helped her to the bathroom, I brought her back to bed and then said I had to run downstairs for a moment. But she didn't want me to leave.

"Will you come up here later and stay with me for a while?"

"Yes," I said.

I called Kathy from downstairs, tears in my voice and hysterical, feeling I was breaking down. I was panicking, like when I told her my mother was dying and what would happen to her over the next few months.

"I can't take care of my mother. It's too much. We have to get a nurse for her today. You know I can't do this to myself. I don't have anybody else. You have to help me. I can't give her what she needs, and I'm falling apart."

She answered by saying:

"I was going to call you. I want you to hire a nurse that I heard of from a friend of mine, who's very good. She could start tomorrow morning and take care of your mother five days a week and some weekends. "

"She'll empty her colostomy bag and catheter, give her pain medication that she can take from bed and leave her some food until she comes the next morning. We're also able to call her, if there's any emergencies."

"Thank God you found someone," I said. "I didn't know what I was going to do."

I calmed down almost as suddenly as I panicked – feeling a little more reassured than I'd felt that Kathy would at least help me take care of some things for my mother. But I probably could only depend on her when I told her that I was in a crisis, like now. How much else could I expect, knowing she couldn't stand my mother?

I went back upstairs to my mother's room to honor her wishes and stay for a while. When I walked in to see her, it was different than when I first saw her. There was pity for her written all across my face. I just wanted to fall to my knees when I saw her nearly confined to her bed, half her normal size, knowing some of her body organs were no longer working and that her suffering was only growing. I stood there speechless, knowing her life would be coming to an end. She stood up in bed as best she could and then said a few things to me.

"You know how much I've loved you."

"Yes, I know, maybe too much," I said.

"Will you move back home and stay with me? I have no one else. You can come and go when you want, but I need to see you every day. Why can't a son be there for his mother, especially now? This isn't how I raised you."

I replied and said:

"I have my own apartment and can't move home. It's better for me not to see you every day and I have to concentrate on work."

"I'll come over at least three times a week. You'll also have a full-time nurse. She'll be here every day of the week, except sometimes not on the weekends."

"She'll give you your pain medication, take you to the bathroom, feed you and empty your colostomy bag and catheter. If there's any side effects from your medications, she'll also help you."

"I still would prefer you being here," she said.

I responded by saying:

"You'll be okay. I've told the nurse that she has to do everything for you, since you're in pain and don't have much strength. You can also call her, if there are any emergencies."

I'll leave her phone number by the nightstand next to your bed. You know I'll be seeing you pretty often."

When I told my mother that she may have loved me "too much," it was intentional to separate myself from the attachment I had for her growing up. Still, even hearing myself say that to her triggered my guilt that I abandoned her when I left home. Those feelings had taken over me when she asked me to move back home and I wouldn't, knowing she didn't have anyone else.

How much I was continuing to fight what often consumed me. I didn't have any self-compassion for myself, being that critical of not doing enough for my mother. There was part of me that didn't even feel human when I refused to move back home – no emotions or feelings, just a son who only cared about himself. How could I continue to live that way? Where was the forgiveness for what my mother had gone through and feeling every bit of compassion in seeing what was happening to her now?

But I needed the distance from her. I couldn't return to the place that I left for a reason. I'd only be coming home out of guilt, not intention. There were also things growing up that my mother had done to me I couldn't overcome, even after I left home. The undeserved rage and bitterness that had never left me for Kathy, hatred for all Germans, the trauma of certain colors and German accents that reminded me of Nazis. I felt going back home and giving my mother what she wanted would also sacrifice the rest of me.

She didn't say anything more when I told her that her love for me may have felt overbearing. How could she? As I've told, she was no different than some survivors, who were that impacted by their trauma from the Holocaust. Sometimes it was manifested by feeling they needed to do everything to protect their children after what they'd been through. One of those ways was being over protective of their children. At times, it probably had to be hurting more than helping them. Some of their kids probably felt like they couldn't breathe.

When I left my mother's, I didn't know why Kathy hadn't purchased groceries for her like she said that she would. She also hadn't shown up again to see her later in the week like I thought she might. I guess she really could only help from a distance. The best example was the only help I had from her was the nurse she found. It was probably too much for her to see my mother more often, given how they couldn't get anywhere near each other all their lives.

Why all of a sudden would I expect her to have compassion for my mother – even knowing she was dying? She had every reason not to have any feelings, if only for the little time my mother had left. Kathy probably couldn't forget their past. But I just hoped despite what she felt, it could be put aside when my mother needed someone the most.

Schindler had put aside the Nazi Party's hatred for Jews that he himself was guilty of for a while, until he saw every bit of their inhuman suffering. That reach of humanity let him save my mother and that many other Jewish lives. Why couldn't my stepmother do that now? I guess I understood, but maybe I didn't. There was no way to really understand what my stepmother couldn't do. I wasn't her and too heavily influenced, seeing what my mother was going through,

I couldn't see my mother again for a week due to a few deadlines for work. It only made me feel more guilty, not seeing her as much as I told her I would. The boundaries I'd set were starting to break down. I didn't even have any compassion for myself that not seeing her the past week was something I couldn't avoid. I just began to feel that my life didn't matter as much as hers.

There was no way I could look at that differently, not seeing her for years and needing to be there for her now far more than I'd ever been. How much I needed Kathy to be there for me right now. While she wasn't a very sensitive person, one of her best qualities was being far more practical than many. I could almost hear her tell me a few things that would give me some perspective.

> "Your mother's going to die, but you have a life ahead of you. You just can't give up yourself for her. She's suffering, but there's not much you can do, except be with her as much as you can."

> "How could you give her much more than that? You have to protect yourself."

The next time I came over to my mothers, I began to do some minor cleaning that I really didn't want to do. I was tired after work and everything in the house was dirty. It turned my stomach. I really didn't know where to begin, or after I cleaned if anything would even look any better. While I was vacuuming, the nurse administered my mother's pain medication, emptied her colostomy bag and massaged her back, legs and arms. Her pain was expanding into many other areas.

The cancer had continued to spread and began to move with speed throughout her body. The little cleaning I did made me feel a little better. But the feelings of helping her and being compassionate didn't last long. I was filled with shame I couldn't do more.

After I finished cleaning, I sat with my mother next to where she was lying in bed. She looked at me with a little smile and I looked at her, but I was doing everything possible not to feel more. If only for a little while, I had to forget everything she was going through, that it was my mother, and at least some of my emotions seeing her in that much pain. I knew that I wouldn't have been able to help her, if I was overcome by how much she was suffering. But I also couldn't watch her lying there for very long, with not much left of her.

No matter what I tried, I was still turning into a mess emotionally. This was probably going to be my life for the next three months – nothing would change. I would give her the compassion that I felt, but punish myself that it wasn't enough. How could my life even move forward after she died? I was consumed, even panicking, over the fear of not getting past living with unrelenting regret about seeing her again only when she was dying.

The irony was that my mother had raised to me always be there for her, but I wouldn't have survived like that. Still, it was eating me up inside that I wasn't there for her the way I felt that I should have been. We were both victims of her trauma from the Holocaust. The only difference was that hers would end, but I didn't know if mine ever would.

When I visited her later in the week, she just stared at me when I walked in her bedroom. She didn't say much, like always these days. It had to be due to feeling that much pain, except the few words that I heard every time I visited. "Don't Leave." I was getting more used to hearing that when I came over. But it still took something out of me. When I'd leave the house, I'd always be thinking, "How could I leave her?"

While I was upstairs, the nurse was in the bathroom emptying my mother's colostomy bag and catheter. She wasn't taking her to wash up any longer, telling me that she was getting too weak and couldn't be moved from her bed anymore. After what she said, I started to even feel more compassion for her. But I had to repress the feelings to remain functional. I'd been seeing everything she was going through and being reminded of my guilt much too often these days, I began to feel my only amends was to stay by her side continuously.

After I was with my mother for about ten minutes, I ran downstairs – when I heard sounds coming from the kitchen. I burst in there and saw pots, pans, dishes and glasses being put away in the cabinets. I heard a scrubbing noise that sounded like the oven being cleaned. When I walked into the kitchen, the refrigerator and the rusted bottom broiler door were open. Once I saw who was cleaning the oven, I was in shock – it was Kathy.

I was overcome with emotion that she was in the kitchen. My jaw felt like it dropped to the floor, and my eyes couldn't have been open wider – feeling amazed that she was there cleaning things. I thought it couldn't be her, after the way she hadn't said much to my mother when she saw her. She didn't even come to visit her again in the past few weeks, like I thought she would.

I finally stepped right next to her, after she'd been cleaning the oven. It was to convince myself that it was actually my stepmother cleaning my mother's kitchen. She opened the refrigerator door to put a fresh loaf of bread in there. I also saw that she removed the uncovered and spoiled food which filled the shelves racks. Then she opened the oven door to put away a couple baking pans under the bottom oven rack.

I just couldn't believe that she cleaned the baked grease and crusted food stains, which lined the top and inside of the oven. She had also put clean glasses, cups and dishes in the cabinets, which probably hadn't been done for years. I finally said to her what I couldn't bring myself to do at first, with my face drawn and stretched to where it nearly hurt. I looked that way from being stunned the moment I saw her in the kitchen.

"I didn't think you really wanted to help me, or my mother, after I called you. You hadn't visited her for more than a week."

In a very angry voice, Kathy replied.

"I really can't see how a person can live like this. She can't do anything for herself. If not me, who else will help her? I know she's not able to count on you very much now."

"You have a job and you've never had to take care of someone who is sick and dying, especially being it's your mother."

"I know you've taken care of your place pretty well, but you wouldn't be able to clean a house with as much filth and dirt as there is here."

"Once I finish cleaning the refrigerator racks and side shelves, will you hand me some of the groceries in the two bags on the kitchen countertop?"

After I handed her the groceries, I asked if I could do anything else.

She replied and said:

"Don't leave, I'll let you know in the next 15 minutes."

After about thirty minutes she let me know what else she wanted. She was busy scrubbing the oven a third time – every inch of surface from top to bottom. It probably hadn't been cleaned in more than ten years, since my mother moved into the house with me and my brother. Kathy finally asked me to put away the rest of the groceries sitting on the countertop and clean the dark soot that stretched over every bit of the kitchen floor.

I knew that she wanted to go upstairs and see my mother. Despite how much she despised my mother, her eyes had watched her lying in bed, barely looking human any longer, suffering relentlessly. As hard and cold as my stepmother was at times, she really couldn't stand to see anyone suffer – especially watching what my mother was going through.

While I had often been ruthless to her growing up, and her to me sometimes, she was there for me in a crisis when I left home. She helped me in ways I never would have expected. As I've said, I was never too certain how much my father would have done. I also couldn't forget how a few years after the assaults by my brother, Kathy still tried to reconcile with him, giving him the Jewish Star of David. She was someone who cared about people, but maybe didn't often show it with words. She was there for others, often more than most, when someone she knew needed help.

I wasn't happy with all of her comments, hearing the judgment in her words, when I first saw her downstairs. It was pretty normal for her to be critical and it just came with the help she gave me after I left home. I wanted to defend myself, particularly telling me I wasn't capable of helping with any of my mother's care or cleaning the house. But I thought better, realizing if we'd had an argument, I'd be afraid she'd leave and tell me that I had to help my mother myself.

There was no question, I wouldn't have been able to do what Kathy did. I was very glad she was there and felt a ton of weight had been lifted off my shoulders. I felt that she would be in charge of my mother's care. She'd be certain the nurse was doing everything she was supposed to and probably could do some things better than her. I know that even included feeding and bathing my mother more regularly. Kathy hadn't liked that I mentioned recently the nurse hadn't helped her wash up in a few days. She always said " cleanliness defined the person you are." I often felt it was more important to her than even health and having money.

She walked upstairs to my mother's room, dressed pretty well as usual and looked better than I would have been after cleaning a disgusting kitchen. I stopped mopping the kitchen floor and also went upstairs to use the bathroom. There was one downstairs, but I really wanted to see if she was talking to my mother.

I didn't even know what they might say to each other. I opened the door, but only halfway not wanting to interrupt them. Kathy was helping my mother untangle the tubes of her catheter. She also moved them to a more comfortable spot of the bed. I told her that my mother couldn't really move, being too weak and in intolerable pain. She was reacting to the cancer spreading everywhere.

After she made my mother more comfortable, she gently turned her over to one side of the bed, so she could replace her pillowcases and bed sheets. They hadn't probably been changed by the nurse in a few days. She also did some minor cleaning of my mother's bedroom, but nothing more. Still, I couldn't even believe what I was seeing after all these years. Kathy had put aside the lifetime of bitterness between them, even if only temporarily, to help my mother when she no longer could do anything for herself.

While she watched everything my stepmother was doing for her, she didn't say a word. Maybe she hadn't been in shock or even fear, being too weak, or couldn't overcome her pain to feel her emotions. What my mother was going through seemed inhuman. I guess she was more than willing to accept the comfort Kathy was giving her, despite coming from her worst enemy, other than the Nazis. My stepmother just couldn't see her lying there, suffering relentlessly, without trying to give her every bit of care and relief she needed, given the little time she had left.

She also helped feed and talked to her for a little while I was up there. They talked about growing up in a war that happened based upon nothing but racism – hatred especially for Jews. It was ethnic cleansing. None of it was real. They would talk about what they did to survive and how much people born after that time never understood what they went through.

My stepmother's obsession for cleanliness and the filth that she'd seen in every room also left her no choice, but to finally clean every part of the house – the kitchen, downstairs bathroom, both bedrooms, the floors and she did some of my mother's laundry. The upstairs bathtub and toilet's surfaces were covered with dark soiled rings that couldn't be cleaned very well. She felt that it was best if they were replaced. She also shopped for more groceries, seeing there wasn't even a scrap of food in the house that wasn't spoiled.

Kathy also bathed my mother in bed, knowing the nurse wasn't doing that often enough. After watching everything she'd been doing for my mother, I knew I had to do more. How could I let the person that my mother felt was her bitter enemy be her primary caretaker and feel I wasn't doing enough. While I was often more worried about protecting myself from guilt than helping her, this was still my mother who was dying in a few months. I was watching her suffer far more than anyone deserved.

Kathy had found compassion for her, feeling that regardless of what happened, she couldn't turn away from someone when they needed her most. Then why couldn't I? That awareness, realizing sometimes helping others is more important than how you may feel about them – even deservedly. It let me begin to do much more than I had within the next few weeks.

But I questioned how this might impact me. I couldn't help myself from being afraid that my past might return. Would I begin to feel the unhealthy attachment to my mother again that I had growing up? It might also perpetuate the guilt that stayed with me when I left home. But it didn't matter – seeing that my stepmother was probably sacrificing herself for my mother, then how could I not as well?

There were things that I felt I couldn't do but did anyways. While Kathy felt it best to replace the bathtub and sink that I also thought looked disgusting, I cleaned them anyways. My mother had never cleaned the refrigerator's freezer, which had things growing in it due to food that hadn't been thrown away in years. I cleaned that as well, even feeling nauseous seeing what was in there

It took hours when I cleaned these things which never had been. But as I mentioned for other stuff that I cleaned in the house, they still never looked much better. But I felt whatever I did was helping my mother. I finally began to feel a little less selfish – not caring about myself as much as I had been. When she became sick, I always only considered how what I was doing for her might impact me.

I wished that I could have known how my mother might have felt, having my stepmother being her primary caretaker. While she didn't say anything, watching what Kathy was doing for her, willing to accept her help, how could she not have been conflicted? Her enemy of a lifetime, finally seeing her at the darkest time of her life after the Holocaust – not having anyone else to give her what she needed. As I've said, despite all the cleaning my stepmother had done in the kitchen, she couldn't have looked much better when she came into my mother's bedroom. That alone might have eaten away at my mother.

But maybe there was a way she could realize what Kathy had to confront, putting aside every bit of her feelings to find compassion for a woman who was dying miserably. Could it change any of her beliefs about my stepmother? Maybe it would let her finally see that Kathy's family weren't Nazis or indifferent as to what happened to Jews in the Holocaust. I wished she'd heard the story that I did – learning that her father was murdered by two Nazis because he wouldn't support fascist ideology and what was happening back then, especially to Jews.

Still there probably wasn't any way that my mother would be able to overcome her trauma after the holocaust. It made her see Kathy not for who she was. I've said she had to have been that traumatized. Her whole family that had been murdered in the Holocaust when she was only a teenager. The happiest years of her life which had been lost living in terror, especially before working for Oskar Schindler. She must have questioned how would she survive being alone in a Nazi concentration camp. But could that world of darkness begin to change – knowing her primary caretaker just months before her death was a German? Would she finally again remember that her fate in the Holocaust was changed by a Nazi?

I'd finally felt more of a difference in my feelings towards Kathy than the past, seeing everything she was doing for my mother. But my feelings towards her still weren't even close to what they needed to be. There was so much bitterness that remained inside me, despite that it was never deserved. What began as a child and penetrated that far within me was too much to overcome. If I could have just known how much of a sacrifice it was for her to put aside everything she felt towards my mother for that long – even knowing that nothing might change between them. I guess she finally decided that she had to be there for her, knowing my mother was going to die in a few months.

If I could have understood how hard it was for her to put aside how she felt about my mother, it would have let me see the person she truly was. Would someone else have been able to do what she did for my mother – being faced with the same conflicted situation? Your worst enemy of the past two decades bitterly dying in front of you? Would you help care for them? There probably wasn't a right answer.

I have felt there could be a parallel drawn in a way to what Schindler did for my mother and how Kathy sacrificed herself for her. He initially exploited Jews by acquiring property they no longer could own under Nazi decrees and having them work for him as cheap labor. But he put aside his capitalist greed once he'd seen the torture and dehumanization of Jews in the Krakow Ghetto and by Amon Goeth in Plaszow.

Schindler sacrificed his wealth and risked his life to save my mother and every other Jewish life he could. How many would have done that for Jewish people during the Holocaust? Kathy also gave my mother what she needed after seeing what she was going through, putting aside a lifetime of the hatred she felt. Both of them did what had to be done – giving her life when she faced death.

When I began seeing my mother a little more frequently, she also stopped by one time with my father. They both came into the house, but she only went upstairs to see my mother. When they first came inside, my father walked into the living room, looked around for a second and then went into the kitchen, but only for a couple minutes. He turned around, walked to where my stepmother was standing by the stairs, looked directly at her and only said a few words.

"I'll wait for you in the car. Don't be long."

They were going to visit some friends and couldn't stay long, but Kathy wanted to check on how my mother was doing. She wanted to see how bad her pain had been, whether her colostomy bag or catheter needed to be emptied, if she needed to eat, or had to be bathed. After my mother told her that she was a little hungry and seeing that she didn't need anything else, she brought her a little bit of food. It was nothing fancy, just a yogurt and a little cereal. The nurse had told us it was getting harder and harder for her to keep anything down. The cancer had spread to her stomach and she was in a lot of pain after she ate.

When Kathy left my mother's bedroom, she thanked her for coming over and bringing something upstairs for her to eat. But she didn't say much else. While they had talked sometimes about things that they had in common, there were also times she didn't say much to her. As the cancer spread, she had to be often overcome by unrelenting pain and probably still didn't know how to react, seeing Kathy being her caretaker.

I couldn't stop feeling disgusted with my father that he didn't even want to see my mother, knowing that she was dying. I didn't even bother saying anything to him, being certain he wouldn't change his mind. I knew that was partially due to an inability to see someone very ill. There was no way he could look at her frailty, nearly emaciated and suffering. He never visited anyone in hospitals, often being afraid that what if their illness happened to him.

But most importantly, I don't think he could reconcile the differences between my mother and him, even temporarily, that led to a marriage with no survivors and a divorce that might have been worse. He also probably couldn't forgive how much she hated him, despite how he felt about her. But even far more, how she felt about my stepmother and what my mother had done to me and my brother.

When my father said to Kathy, "Don't be long," I felt it was due to not understanding how she could be there for my mother, even now, knowing how much she despised her. That probably couldn't have been more apparent than the two times my brother attacked her. As I'd said, my father always felt my mother made him do them, knowing how much vengeance she had towards Kathy.

I knew how much he couldn't stand my mother, especially when they talked briefly after Harry attacked Kathy physically, saying that he'd destroy her if anything else happened to his wife. His insensitivity towards my mother was also probably being angry – feeling Kathy betrayed him by helping her . I'm certain he couldn't believe everything she was doing for her. It had to have been too hard for him to understand, believing that she still felt the same way about my mother as he did.

I also saw what little feelings my father had for her from what I heard him say to Kathy. It was after she left my mother's and was getting in their car. He didn't ask her how she was feeling, how she looked, or if they talked about anything. All he said was, "Why did you take so long? You know we're going to be late to see Sam and Frima." How she responded to what he said I'd never forget.

> "I know what she did to you and Morrie, but I can't watch her suffering like this now. There's nobody else to help her. Not like what I can do."

> "You know that it's always been my nature to help people when they need me. She has to know that she has someone. It can't change what we've gone through, but it makes me feel a little better."

My father didn't really say anything else. They left and went to see their friends. Both of them always deeply spoke their minds and she clearly told him what had to be said. But there were times he wouldn't bother to say anything more to her when they didn't agree on something. He was a little afraid of her. Still, that couldn't have been easy for her to say to him. As I'd said, they always agreed on how they felt about my mother and even more importantly couldn't forget what she did to her kids.

Kathy told me that my father would never forgive my mother for wanting me to feel every bit of her hatred for him, let alone what she did to my brother. He also was probably that angry at her for everything she was doing for my mother, probably often reminding her not to forget why they felt about her the way they did.

In the next few weeks, I was doing more for my mother than I'd ever thought was possible. I would visit her at least four times a week, clean some of the house and spend a few hours with her. We didn't say much to each other. I was scared she'd want to talk about the past, knowing I left home to forget about that part of my life. I couldn't return to feeling her unrelenting hatred again like I did growing up, that I still felt sometimes.

If we talked about that time, especially my childhood, it probably would have triggered even more guilt than I had felt the past few months. Those feelings I was being reminded of too often these days. The emotions that let me feel I abandoned her when I left home and being ashamed not to see her again until I knew that she might be dying.

While I was giving my mother what I felt she needed, I couldn't do other things – like balancing that well with work. I was in a newer position that was demanding, being a manager, and it was one of our busiest times of the year. There were times I just stared at my computer for a couple hours in the day watching the screen saver. It was a landscape with endless trees, sitting in the valley of a stunning mountain range. But the serenity didn't prevent me from dwelling on what my mother was going through. I had never known a person who was dying, let alone being my mother.

Sometimes at work, I even questioned my humanity and values for a mother that was dying. Despite spending more time with her, I was often ashamed, feeling that I still didn't have enough compassion. I felt that at least I should have talked with her more, seeing her lying in bed with no hope. Maybe what I felt was purely survivor's guilt, knowing that she never had much of a life, but after leaving home I did.

I would often sit for hours with my manager John telling him about my mother's condition – seeing her turning into a skeleton, watching the unrelenting suffering and how I wasn't coping, facing my mother dying. John was someone from the moment I met him, who was pretty emotional. I felt that I could talk to him about what I was going through.

When I first met him, he spent an hour talking to me about work and life balance and how the most important thing in anyone's life was "What Do You Want to Be Remembered For?" This was a quote I once heard from a highly regarded therapist who wanted me to consider her perspective on the meaning of life. They were words that I'd never forget.

John thought I needed to get more in touch with my feelings than I had been for my mother. But he didn't know that it was wrecking my mind. I really thought that I'd lose my job, getting further and further behind at work. But he'd work through the night if he needed to. I couldn't work overtime much, spending more and more time with my mother.

It was my stepmother again who helped me when I couldn't help myself. Somehow after listening to enough of what she told me, it let me get back to focusing on work, despite how much I'd been trapped in my guilt. She would repeatedly tell me things which finally helped me realize I didn't have to suffer like I was.

> "You can't lose your whole life over her now. There really isn't much you can do anyways."

"I know it's very hard to manage what your feeling – understanding that it's your mother who's dying. But your whole life is in front of you and just can't give it all up. I won't let you."

After what Kathy said, I didn't even know how much I needed to thank her for what she'd told me. Her advice helped me not come apart at a time I thought it might be inevitable. But I still wasn't able to tell her what she deserved to hear – thanking her with every bit of my heart for what she'd done for me. I wasn't even able to let her know how what she said helped me get back to my life.

How would I ever be able to finally detach from my mother's perceptions? It's what I could never do, being left the victim since childhood. I didn't have the vision to see Kathy differently than my mother did. What I'd been told, despite that it was never real had stayed with me for a lifetime.

It was now early March. February had been the slowest, most painful month of my life, as I watched my mother continue to die. One day Kathy and I had both been over at my mother's, and she told me that my brother called my dad. He was living at a halfway house in Uptown – Wilson Manor. He hadn't lived at home in years. Harry told my father that he wanted to visit my mother. He also told him that he wanted to move back home.

She and I had decided not to tell him that my mother was dying. We were too afraid of how he might react – due to his chronic mental condition. But we needed to tell her that he wanted to see her, though not that he wanted to move back home. Despite his mind no longer really being there, he was still her son and they'd lived together for some time after I left home. We felt that gave her the right to decide if she wanted to see him. But we didn't know what she'd even say.

My mother hadn't mentioned him once since we began to see her. After deciding that I'd tell her my brother wanted to visit – feeling it best coming from her other son – we came into her room and sat down next to where she was lying in bed. I said that I had to tell her something.

> "Harry talked to dad for a couple minutes and he said that he wanted to see you. He said that he hadn't seen you in four months, since he went to Wilson Manor, and needed to see you right away. Dad told me he's pretty upset that he hasn't been able to see you."

My mother responded and said:

> "He must never come back here again. I can't be near him. You don't know what he can do and I can't help him anymore. Please don't let me see him. There's not much left of me, and I couldn't take seeing him. Aren't I suffering enough?"

I replied by saying:

> "Mom, I had to tell you that he wants to see you. He's your son. But I understand what you said, and we'll be certain he doesn't come here."

"You know he won't take no for an answer. But he doesn't have a key and wont be able to get in the door."

It had to be heartbreaking to see your son mentally ill, let alone when you're dying. But I had a feeling there was something else inside her that didn't want to see him again. After I left home, when my brother wasn't in psychiatric hospitals or a halfway house, I was pretty certain there were things that happened between them I didn't want to know.

Harry had a very bad temper. He might have inherited that from my father. That's what my mother and Kathy said about my dad's anger more than a few times. While my mother knowingly was controlling. I felt that my brother had to have beaten her up when I left home, at least a few times. He probably reacted hostilely to some things she demanded. There had to have been times he wouldn't let himself be subdued by her, despite how much we were growing up.

I also felt pretty certain there was an incestuous relationship between them. But I didn't really know who was the perpetrator or whether it was consensual. She may not have wanted anything to happen – especially if he aggressively pursued her and forced the relationship between them. Or my mother may have forced the relationship on him due to that much control over his mind, but didn't want to remember what she'd done. I don't know why, but this was even more disgusting than Harry beating her up to understand.

Even before I left home, I thought there might have been an intimate relationship going on between them. I still wasn't really certain that something happened back then, considering I went away to college the fall before I moved out and wasn't home very much my senior year of high school. But neither of them, from what I knew had a sexual relationship or dated anyone, at least in my final year of high school, and after I left home. It's also why I stayed as far away as I did when I moved out. I was too afraid to get anywhere near them and ask either one if there had been any physical abuse or a sexual relationship between them.

I didn't even feel there was therapy that could have helped me confront what might have happened. It was the early 1980's, and I didn't know of any help for victims of these things, let alone the family members who knew about them. Still, I might have tried to do something, if I'd known what happened – knowing how unsafe and sick this was, and even how it might impact me.

I didn't tell Kathy anything pertaining to what I felt. I didn't think it was necessary and honestly I was embarrassed. But considering that Harry was mentally unstable, neither had an intimate relationship in years and telling her they were always together after I left, she must have had some of the same suspicions.

When I thought about what probably happened between them, it let me realize again how fortunate I was for leaving home – knowing what happened between them could have been my fate. I'd be the shadow of my brother. Someone that was ruined by a mother who never really understood everything that she'd done to him.

But even knowing what I escaped, I still couldn't really see what Kathy had helped me not have to go through. To see her differently, there probably had to be something I wouldn't expect or could do myself that would change how I felt. I've probably said too many times, my feelings towards her had just lasted way too long.

My brother did come over to my mother's house a few times after Kathy and I knew that he wanted to see her. Fortunately, we were both there and didn't let him inside. We weren't surprised when he came over. He rang the doorbell, but we couldn't look to see who was there. The whole door was solid wood and couldn't tell who was standing outside.

I don't know why, but we didn't ask who was there when he rang the bell. After he pushed it far too many times, which sounded like piercing carnival bells, we finally opened the door. He asked to see my mother, but we told him that she wasn't feeling well and couldn't see him right now. He didn't take what we told him very well. In seconds, he pushed the door from where he was standing outside with all his strength and shouted hysterically – "You'd better let me in right now, otherwise I don't know what I'll do."

Harry was pretty strong when he became enraged, but somehow we held him back from coming in the house. Still, he didn't leave right away and remained standing in front of the door for a while, but didn't say anything. Kathy told him angrily that if he didn't leave, we'd call the police and they'd arrest him. I also yelled to him with a hostile tone, that if he didn't leave he'd never see my mother again. After what we said, he finally left.

There was also a second time my brother came over a few weeks later. When he rang the bell this time, we asked who was there. He said it was "Harry and I want to see my mother." But we didn't say another word, while he just stood by the door for probably another 10 minutes, before he finally left. We were a little afraid that he'd continue coming back, worried that he'd forget we didn't let him in the house when he came over. His memory was gone and he was pretty delusional from having schizophrenia. I guess, luckily after what happened we did something that must have worked, and he didn't come over again.

Near the end of March, Kathy called me and said that given that my mother would probably die in another month, we needed to determine right away if she had a will. We had to know if her assets would be protected not to have to go through probate. I certainly didn't have any experience with a will or estate planning. How did I know how to protect someone's assets after they die? I was just 25.

Kathy mentioned when we talked that she knew my mother was very cheap. I listened to her also tell me a few things.

> "She must have saved every penny of alimony your father had given her and I'm pretty certain she has plenty of assets. They're probably all in her name. But seeing that nothing is organized when I come over, I'm certain she doesn't have a will to take care of these things. If there's no will, you or Harry wouldn't be beneficiaries of her assets."

> "Her estate would go through probate and I've seen illegitimate claims filed for what's owned where people lose everything. I then told her that we needed to protect what she had, but I didn't know how."

I further said:

> "I know the house was never put in a trust. How do we that? I'm not certain what to do. I've never had any experience with a person in my family dying and managing the responsibilities for their affairs when they pass away."

> "Will you please help me? I don't want to have someone take her assets – if the house isn't in a trust and she doesn't have a will."

> "You're right, she never spent any money and what she has took many years to save. I don't want to see it all gone."

"I need the money for my future and Harry will certainly need some for psychiatric hospitals and halfway houses that aren't covered by Medicaid or Medicare, I'm sure as he gets older."

Kathy replied by saying:

"We have to first move her savings accounts into both of your names in the next few weeks. I know she has several accounts, but that can be done very fast."

"We'll have to get her to sign a power of attorney to manage her affairs. It protects us legally for doing things with her consent."

"We have to go to every one of her five banks next week and request joint account cards for her to sign. The accounts will then be in both your names."

"You'll be able to withdraw money from the accounts, but don't take anything out yet without telling me."

"You've never had a lot of money yourself, but I managed your father's money that he earned from his business."

"If not for me, he would have spent every dime he made. Your mother knows I know how to take care of money. Your father said she even told that to him once."

"She might think that since you didn't have a lot yourself and still being pretty young, you'd spend what she left you foolishly. I need to tell her you'll manage what you inherit responsibly."

We went to all five of my mother's banks during the next two weeks to get account cards for my mother to sign. How difficult would that be, knowing she might not trust me? I hadn't seen her before she was sick for the past seven years. I certainly wasn't expecting her to trust my stepmother. Kathy and I would also have to discuss with a woman that was dying transferring her assets, living with intolerable suffering. It was clearly understandable that we might not be able to reason with my mother, knowing what she was going through.

Each time I'd go into one of the banks and ask for the account cards, I'd feel guilty. The money in the bank accounts was roughly $75,000 (certainly worth a good deal more today) and just be in my name once my mother died. There was part of me that was drowning in guilt - feeling I didn't deserve what she'd be leaving me. I can't say enough how much guilt I often felt after I left home and hadn't seen my mother again until I knew she might be that sick. But I did feel a little better telling Kathy how I felt and having her reassure me I was doing what had to be done.

I called Kathy the day before we would see my mother to discuss how we'd convince her to let me be a joint owner of her assets. We had to consider my mother might not trust either of us, saved every dime, or she might feel that she was letting go of everything she had - knowing some holocaust survivors, including my mother often feared everything they owned might be taken from them. That consumed me not knowing how she agreed to anything, even to protect her assets.

After discussing what we'd we would tell my mother, Kathy felt it was best if she was the one talking to her. With her being older, she'd better know what to say to her. I was also glad she knew people who had gone through this in the past. When we talked, she told me that she'd tell her, if the assets weren't held jointly, she might lose them to claims for debts that people believed were due to them. She'd mention that they're often filed by anyone against an estate and sometimes aren't even legitimate. People will file them when they know there's assets to see if they can get any money.

In fact, she'd tell my mother a story of one of her friends, who had a million-dollar estate that was in her friend's name. She was widowed with three teenagers. All the money that she'd left for her kids was gone after she died due to claims filed in probate that were in excess of the estate. I also listened to what else she planned to say when we went to see my mother.

> "If you love your kids, wouldn't you want them to have money for their future, particularly Harry? He'll never work again and needs to be taken care of."

> "The money for him will be used for things like when he needs to be in psychiatric institutions – particularly halfway houses, or permanent facilities and buying him clothes. He's covered by Medicaid, but most places are very expensive."

"The ones they pay for aren't specialized facilities and don't offer long-term inpatient care."

"You want him to stay at a decent facility. If he doesn't have anything, they'll just put him somewhere for probably up to a month and then he'll be on the street."

If my mother trusted Oskar Schindler, a Nazi to save her life, why couldn't she trust us? I felt we were there for her when she needed someone most (obviously except during the Holocaust). But I understood why I couldn't expect my mother to feel differently – knowing everything that happened to her. How she felt about Kathy probably hadn't changed much, despite what she was doing for her, and I hadn't talked to her in years.

CHAPTER VIII

Hope Is the Last to Die

As planned, Kathy and I went to see my mother the next day to convince her to ultimately give me control of her assets. When we came over and were going upstairs to her bedroom, I repeatedly told Kathy that I didn't feel this would turn out like we wanted, questioning if she'd trust us. I really had to be honest and tell her that I was doubtful whether any of my mother's bitterness for her worst enemy in my lifetime had changed, even if only a little. She had to feel at least to some extent that my mother's hatred, which possessed her, probably was too much to change.

I also was pretty anxious as to whether my mother had gotten over at least some bitterness I felt she might have had for me. How could she forgive me – not having seen her in that many years, until knowing that she might be dying? There was also a real uneasiness about how she may have felt when I told her that I wouldn't move back home, despite watching everything she was going through.

I never really knew her feelings towards my stepmother or myself after we began taking care of her, since she didn't share them with us. Other than when she talked to Kathy about how they grew up, she didn't say much or have any reaction to both of us being there. Again, maybe that was being in shock sometimes that my stepmother was really her caretaker, or often being overcome by the uncontrollable pain she often felt.

But despite what I said to Kathy she still felt that my mother would listen to what she had to say. There was also one thing she said to me that I hadn't even considered. How much they talked when they were together.

"Hasn't she been letting me do everything for her? We also talk plenty when I spend time with her. You might know that we've talked for hours about how we grew up in a war. One that never made any sense."

"We tell each other, people who didn't go through what we did can't understand the family we lost and how grateful we are to live in a free country."

"But we never talk much about life after the Holocaust in America. You know that wouldn't be much good."

I was in shock when I first knew how much they were talking, and that they had found something in common. Who could believe that after that many years of hatred between them that this could ever happen?

Still, I was doubtful that the discussion of giving up any control of her assets would go well. My mother's money was her security. It couldn't be separated from her – like it was attached to her heart. No one else could touch it, even if it was only to protect what she had. I guess feeling that way was probably due to how the Nazis took everything from her family. The money and assets that would've totaled over $1M today.

As I'd mentioned, there were many Holocaust survivors who had the same feelings. How could you blame them? The Nazis took everything they had, especially from Jews without a reason. They would throw their belongings out the windows of their homes and confiscated their money when they deported them to the ghettos and concentration camps.

When Kathy and I walked into my mother's room, my heart was pounding. It was racing like it might even stop beating. My hands were slippery from the sweat of anxiety that I could barely tolerate. I didn't feel my mother wouldn't only trust us, but that she might even tell us to leave. We were asking for her to have faith in us with her money. We saw my mother lying in bed, in her blue velvet robe that she loved Kathy purchased for her.

She was maybe 75 pounds, nearly a skeleton, and yellow color filled her cheeks and hands as jaundice penetrated through her veins. Her beautiful thick brown hair was now only meager, coarse white strands.

We sat down next to her bed and asked how she was feeling. She didn't say much, except "not very good." How much else could she say, with all of her suffering? Her medication was no longer able to control the pain much. She looked at us with the whitest, pale brown eyes, as the cancer had continued spreading. She was probably coming to accept that her fate was near. We told her that we wanted to know whether she had a will when the time would come. Her reply was cold, and hard to hear.

"No, I will donate all my money to the Ark," she said.

But I wasn't too surprised to hear that. The Ark is a non-profit agency helping Jews in the Chicago community in need of free services, supporting those who face many hardships. They provide help for people in need with financial, employment and medical issues. It's an organization aligned with Jewish laws and values.

Kathy replied by saying:

> "Rose, you can't do that. Your kids will have nothing. I can't really believe that's what you want for them. What about their future?"

My mother responded and said:

> "They haven't been there for me for a long time. I know you both helped me, since I became sick, but I've been alone for many years."

> "Bobby left me when he was 18 and only began seeing me again when I became sick. You know that Harry hasn't been well for over 10 years. I've had nothing from them."

Kathy replied by saying:

> "Rose, I know we've always had our bitter differences, especially in terms of what you feel I did to you all these years. I know you'll probably never get over what you believe Morrie did to you when he left you."

> "But I want what is best for you and both your children. I hope you can realize that, especially after the time we've been spending together."

> "Bobby is your only healthy son and he really does love you. I know that's true. He only left home because he was terrified that he'd wind up like his brother."

"If he hadn't moved out, there probably would have been nothing left of him. He would have become just like Harry. Is that really what you would have wanted?"

"You know that he will never get well. He can't live by himself and Bobby will see that the money he'll get is used to take care of him. He doesn't have private insurance, only Medicaid."

"He'll buy him clothes and use the money for things like maybe better halfway houses than Medicaid will cover or if he's able to get him into permanent psychiatric institutions.

"The better halfway houses are very expensive, and I know he'll do what he can for him."

"Hopefully the places for more permanent care will still take him, you know he doesn't like to be locked up and often finds a way to run away from them."

"Harry doesn't have much from his life, why wouldn't you want that for him?"

"Bobby also deserves some money for his future, especially if he gets married, has kids and maybe buys a home."

"As you know, things are very expensive these days and even a good job won't pay for everything. Shouldn't there be some money for his future?"

"I know you saved everything Morrie gave you. You didn't even spend anything on yourself. But does Bobby deserve to live like you did?"

"You know I am very good with managing money. I'll see to it that he spends what you leave him for what's necessary."

"I won't let him waste it on crazy things and you have my word that as long as I live, what you've given him will be spent wisely. Rose, you need to trust me."

Kathy finished talking to my mother and she asked us to help her sit up in bed. She could no longer do that by herself. She looked at both of us that peacefully, despite her frailty and unrelenting suffering, with a smile that touched me. It penetrated into every bit of my heart. After what Kathy was doing for my mother, I felt that she also really wanted what was best for her.

The bitterness between her and my mother that had lasted my whole life must have finally been changing. After not having shared her feelings towards us when she became sick, maybe we finally knew some of what she felt. There was also a certain trust that I was shocked to see by the way my mother looked right at us. Nothing like that had ever happened before, after we began to take care of her. She was willing to hear what Kathy had to say.

"Thank you. I'll listen to what you want me to do."

Kathy said:

"You have to agree to let Bobby be listed jointly with you on all your bank accounts, the house and whatever stocks you own. If not, once you pass away, your assets will go to probate."

"In probate, there are claims filed by people who feel you owe them money, and some aren't even legitimate. Sometimes they're filed when people learn someone dies, hopefully to get some money."

"The claims may decrease what have you left for Harry and Bobby. Or you may risk losing all your assets."

"I know your health insurance didn't cover everything and maybe you weren't certain if all your hospital bills would be covered when you became sick."

"There may also be claims filed from work I know you did for your house a few years ago. I heard you disputed some of what was done and didn't know if anything had been settled."

"In fact, one of my friends, who had a $1 million of assets and three teenagers had nothing left for them after she died. It was due to claims by people in probate who said they had unpaid debts."

"The debts that people claimed were greater than the value of her assets. I heard there were more than a few claims that weren't even legitimate."

"I know you wouldn't want that to happen to your kids."

My mother sat in bed, looked directly at Kathy after what she told her and shook her head a few times.

"I can't do that to them."

I was ecstatic that she agreed with what Kathy said. It let me feel that she trusted us and knew we were doing what needed to be done. But I just hoped the guilt that I felt sometimes of what I'd be inheriting not being deserved; somehow would get easier. I needed to convince myself we weren't taking anything away from her.

Kathy also discussed plans with my mother for her funeral. It was best she was discussing them with her and not me. I really couldn't. I had never faced the death of a loved one, let alone that of my mother. How could I discuss that with her? I hadn't seen her again for so long, until I knew she might be dying, and then we'd discuss planning her funeral – the ceremony for her actual death.

My decision took into consideration what I'd mentioned that might affect anyone near them who was dying, but also the guilt that I couldn't confront. I had only come to see her again not because I wanted to be with her, but because I felt guilty. I had to see her, knowing she might be that sick. I felt that I wouldn't be able to ever forgive myself if I didn't.

My stepmother had talked to her with a kindness I wouldn't have expected. She was doing everything that she could for my mother. How could she not begin to care about her? But the way she never expressed compassion for others, a lifetime of unconscionable hatred between them and uncertain if she'd actually reconciled her feelings, I saw her kindness as shocking.

> "Rose, I have something else to discuss with you and it's not an easy subject. But, I can handle everything if you prefer. I just want what's best for you."

My mother replied and asked,

> "What are you saying?

Kathy responded with,

> "When the time comes, I don't believe you have plans for your funeral? You didn't pay for a plot in a cemetery and haven't purchased a headstone?"

My mother answered:

> "No, I don't have any plans for when I'm no longer here."

I couldn't believe she said that to Kathy very calmly – not even a bit panicked that she was talking about her death. I was shocked by her subtlety, knowing she'd probably die in the next month. If I had to confront dying, especially knowing there wasn't much time left, I didn't know how I could. But my life was only just beginning, with so much I felt in front of me. Her life had no mercy. She repeatedly had to confront tragedy. Maybe being that calm was accepting her fate, realizing the life she had and being a little older.

Kathy told my mother that she would help her with all the arrangements for the funeral. My mother said she wanted to be buried in Westlawn Cemetery, near my father's mother – Mindel Don - because of how much she loved her. Of course, it was a Jewish cemetery. As I'd told, my grandmother had nearly forced my father to marry her. My mother knew how hurt she was when my father left her, especially for someone who was German and not Jewish.

Kathy also asked her which Rabbi she wanted for her funeral service and what words were to be written on her tombstone. She told her Rabbi Schusterman, who was the rabbi my mother loved from Bnai Ruven, an Orthodox synagogue, where I finished Hebrew school and had my Bar Mitzvah. He also presided over the ceremony.

When I was growing up, my mother would often come to see him. He would listen to her talk for hours about the Holocaust and when the memories became too much, she'd cry about everything that she went through back then. Her family that was taken from her, being only a teenager, and what she had to live through and seen done to other people during the darkest chapter of humanity. She always had to ask him, "Who could do this to people?" And "How come no one stopped them?" He had no direct answers, but he always told her that no matter what, "Hashem (G-d) gives us what we need."

I knew Kathy had never planned any of the traditions in her life for a Jewish funeral. I told her for my mother's tombstone to include that she was the daughter of her parents with their Hebrew names (Zwi & Rifka). I knew she also wanted it to say that she was the mother of two children. After that she didn't care what else was written.

My mother wanted the tombstone to include her parents with their Hebrew names because she wanted a traditional Jewish funeral. I knew it had to be that way for her, knowing she was raised in an Orthodox family before the Holocaust. As I'd probably told, she also returned to strict religious observance after my father left her, until my brother got sick when I was 13. Kathy then looked at my mother again, with a serious and loving voice.

"Rose, you know I'll honor your wishes. You have my word. I want what's best for you and feel I always have. But I understand, if you still don't feel the same way"

Kathy and my mother continued talking for a little bit longer, as we sat next to her bed and she signed the necessary documents for her assets to be owned jointly by both of us. My mother told her that she could never trust anyone with her money. She said, how could I after the Nazis took everything from my family and all Jewish people for themselves?

But Kathy told her that growing up in the war, her family also didn't have much. Everything was used for the war effort. The Nazis could have cared less about the German people. No one really had anything except of course Hitler, the people in his government and the Nazi military. Even when you supported the Nazis, but weren't soldiers fighting the war, you had gornisht – nothing. People didn't have food or clothes and many homes were bombed in the war. We were always plenty grateful that we even had a place to live. The only other things they discussed were a little more about the funeral plans.

I've often felt after that day, seeing my mother confiding in Kathy – telling her she could never trust anyone until now – that Oskar Schindler was in the room. He was telling my mother and every other one of the Jewish lives he saved, who were his employees, that he would look out for them. They would never again live the way they had been – feeling unconscionable suffering and being in fear every day that they would lose their lives. His Jewish workers – in particular, Rena Ferber

After they talked, Kathy put the documents that my mother signed in her purse. Somehow with the little strength she had, suddenly sat back up against the wall in her bed and looked at my stepmother and I. She said just a few words to Kathy. But they would never mean more to me.

"I should have made Shimmas (Shimas means "peace" in Yiddish) with you years ago." Her words couldn't have been said in a softer, subtler and more genuine voice.

"Rose, thank you," Kathy replied. "I too wish everything would have been different between us. I know that what happened in your past is more than most people could understand. Honestly, I'll never really know how much that impacted you."

We sat in silence for the rest of the visit after what they said to each other. My mother was probably four weeks away from dying and didn't really have the strength to talk anymore. But she had told Kathy what she finally needed to tell her and what she couldn't have done before. My stepmother didn't say anything else because she was a person who channeled all her compassion by doing things. She gave my mother a little bit to eat and her pills, rubbed her back and neck for a while, emptied her colostomy bag, said goodbye to us and then left.

But I knew that what my mother said meant a lot to her and felt pretty certain she'd also reconciled at least some of her feelings towards my mother. There also had to have been warmth for Kathy she never would have expected from herself. When my stepmother told her that she understood what happened in her past, it seemed she had that much sensitivity for what my mother went through. After a lifetime of hatred, I was stunned seeing every bit of compassion between them. It was to a reach that I'd never seen before.

"In the Midst of Darkness," I heard such peace and reconciliation in what my mother said to Kathy after all these years. Her words began to change everything in me that I felt towards my stepmother and how I felt about all Germans. I thought my feelings would remain with me for a lifetime. I suddenly saw Kathy, sitting there next to my mother, with a new lens – a warmth that I'd never known, acceptance for her and how much I valued everything she'd done for me and my mother the past few months. I no longer saw her as the Shiksa or the Deichke.

In that moment, I badly wanted to say something to Kathy about how I felt, but I didn't have the right words to say. Still, I wanted to tell her that my feelings towards her had changed before my mother died. I was certain it would mean something to her when they spent time together – maybe it would let her reconcile some of the hatred for my mother that probably still wasn't resolved before she'd die.

I wasn't only able to finally reconcile my feelings towards Kathy, but I also felt differently about my mother. It let me see that she was sorry for what she had done to her, which had traumatized me and ruined my brother. My mother had held others accountable, most notably my stepmother, for the actions of others who were the guilty – the perpetrators and those that were indifferent to the persecution and genocide of the Holocaust. In knowing what my mother had gone through, and finally no longer seeing Kathy as an enemy, but maybe a friend, I knew the way her past impacted her couldn't be helped.

But there was a part of me that still blamed her for how much my brother and I were impacted by hatred growing up. Maybe some of that could have been reconciled, if she didn't only feel remorse towards my stepmother, but also for what she did to us growing up. While things for me had now changed towards my mother, I wished she'd told me that she was actually sorry for what she'd done to us.

Still how could I expect that much from her? She was dying, barely able to move and no longer able to tolerate her pain. Her mind also couldn't function well. I guess it was too much to also hear some words of forgiveness from her for what she did to her kids. Still, it was truly unforgettable that I heard what she said to Kathy before she died. Nothing else would have changed things for me.

I'm certain it meant so much to my mother and also myself that Kathy was honoring her wishes for a traditional Jewish funeral. After the many years of despise between a German and Jew, Kathy had also moved past any racial barriers between them. I guess despite her being married to my Jewish father, there still were walls between the two different cultures. But it was a fitting way for my mother to be leaving the world, knowing that people can come together and overcome what pulls them apart.

The only question that lingered is why I could never see that what my mother told me wasn't real. The hatred that had penetrated inside every bit of me for Kathy, that never left only changed when my mother was able to look at her differently. I needed her acceptance to change my feelings towards my stepmother.

Even after I heard that Kathy's family couldn't stand what the Nazis did to Jews during the Holocaust, and her father was murdered for standing up for what he believed in, it didn't change what I felt. I was conditioned by my mother's perceptions growing up, being a victim since childhood. How can you not be more vulnerable when you're that young and can only believe what your mother is telling you? You don't have any frame of reference to see otherwise.

The change in how I felt about my mother also began to resolve some of the guilt that often consumed me over her. I blamed myself less for feeling that I abandoned her – not seeing her again until I knew that she might be dying. I no longer doubted that leaving home was a choice; it was for survival. The betrayal I also felt leaving my mother when her mental health and my brother's was spiraling – while getting to know to her worst enemy – no longer haunted me. I couldn't see Kathy anymore as my mother's bitter enemy, who I'd felt helped me abandon my mother.

My stepmother and I met two weeks before my mother passed away to arrange her funeral plans. We met with Rabbi Schusterman to perform the funeral services that Kathy promised her, and she purchased a plot for her grave.

I knew that he had to be the one who presided over my mother's funeral. He was the ears for her stories of the Holocaust that she confided in probably more than anyone else. The one who she cried to remembering what people were trying to live through within a genocide. Her tears became endless when she told also told him of her parents and six brothers and sisters that were taken from her only being an older child.

But there was also the hatred that she shared with him for all Germans, who she felt were responsible. Those besides the persecutors – everyone else who she felt was indifferent to what was happening. She always asked him and I, "How could they not have done anything to rescue Jews from what the Nazis were doing to them?" But not every other German was indifferent or accepted the dehumanization of Jewish people. How I wish she would have told me the story of Oskar Schindler. Still, she always blamed both the innocent and the guilty.

I knew that he needed to hear my mother had finally found peace with her worst enemy of a lifetime – a few weeks before she died. I wanted him to know that she'd reconciled all the years of hatred for someone that was never deserved. How could that not matter that much to him? He'd listened to the bitterness that possessed her since I could remember for those who weren't the guilty. He'd probably even heard her rage to a level maybe that he couldn't bear anymore.

When I told him of the reconciliation that she could never find before, he also had to see the inner peace that would carry her soul after she passed away. She had finally understood the words that he repeatedly told her, "That Hashem Always Gives Us What We Need", when he couldn't answer her questions for what allowed the inhumanity of the Holocaust.

The day my mother found peace with my stepmother – not only her, but the Rabbi would know that she could die honoring a sacred conviction. The commitment to uphold one of the most treasured Jewish values – not to hate – which she couldn't tell me and my brother enough growing up doesn't only apply to Jewish people, but to everyone. While the heartbreaking reality was how we grew up differently.

When I saw Kathy and we were going into one of the places to look for tombstones, she was wearing a green colored outfit. The green slacks and jacket she wore were the reed green of the Nazis' military uniforms. It was the same shade of green as her dress that she'd worn the first time I went to my father and stepmother's house for dinner.

As I've told, I was traumatized since childhood by anyone dressed in reed green, those who spoke German or had German accents, white colors or when someone took a large step forward – feeling like they were marching. It reminded me of Nazis. The trauma was all due to growing up hearing my mother's stories of the concentration camps, her family having been murdered in Auschwitz and often saying that all Germans were members of Nazi party, or they didn't care about what was happening to Jews in the Holocaust.

But when I saw Kathy's outfit that day, it was the first time that I wasn't terrified by that shade of green. There was a real feeling I'd turned past the darkness not only for her, but as I'd said maybe all Germans from the peace my mother found. I was filled with hope that color of green and the other things which reminded me of the Holocaust no longer would sometimes traumatize me. I might not even be terrified anymore if I watched Hogan's Heroes, like when I was a kid – often fixated on the Nazi prison guards uniforms that triggered nightmares of my mother's concentration camp stories.

My mother went into a coma in the afternoon the day before she died. I rushed home from work when her nurse called and told me she was no longer conscious. Terminal cancer patients in their final stage of the disease will often go into a coma before they die. She had previously been in hospice for three days, but stayed in the house. Her doctor had to prescribe maximum doses of morphine for her unconscionable pain. She couldn't even say anything to us anymore. Still, there was a glowing warmth in her eyes. I could tell how much comfort she felt knowing that we were there.

When the ambulance picked her up, they brought her to Swedish Covenant Hospital in Chicago's Albany Park neighborhood. She asked us to take her there if she had to be taken to the hospital before she died. When my mother first came to America with my father, they lived in Albany Park and always went to that hospital. I guess it just reminded her of life with my father before everything that happened between them.

Kathy and I decided to drive together to Swedish Covenant and arrived by 3:15 PM. I certainly wasn't in great shape to drive there by myself. Once I knew she was unconscious and probably would die in hours, I couldn't think straight anymore, being overcome by my nerves. I panicked like when I was a kid, when she wasn't home and I didn't know where she was. But my stepmother wasn't impacted like I was. While she wanted to be there for me and my mother, Kathy wasn't family and she probably hadn't resolved everything that happened between them.

We went up to her room and saw her lying in bed with the blue robe Kathy purchased for her. She loved that robe so much and wanted to be buried in it. We both stood and looked at her for a few minutes. Then Kathy sat in a chair next to her towards the end of the bed, while I remained standing, holding her hand and just feeling stunned, looking at her body. She was maybe 65 pounds, just bones, barely any flesh – visibly emaciated. She had lost probably another 10 pounds in the past two weeks.

My mother's eyes were closed, with no life-saving machines assisting her. Kathy and I hadn't discussed with her whether she wanted life support when the time came. I had medical power of attorney and decided that when she was no longer conscious, I didn't want her to be resuscitated. While I didn't know what she preferred, I couldn't see her living like that.

We looked at her hands and face being discolored and painted bright yellow due to the jaundice that often inflicts those with cancer. One of her doctors told me a few days earlier jaundice had thoroughly penetrated into all of the blood inside her body. When I looked at her eyes being closed, I knew she was resting peacefully. Every bit of pain I'd seen in her – the inhuman suffering was finally gone.

I looked over at Kathy and sat down next to her and we both just stared at my mother in silence. We felt that we had done what we needed to for her. Kathy shook her head a couple times when she looked at my mother, but didn't say anything else. Maybe she felt sorry for me and my mother. She probably had some feelings of pity for her that she never had much from her life and it was coming to an end.

She may have also felt compassion for me that I was losing my mother – seeing that I was still attached to her in certain ways. How much clearer had that been than the guilt she often saw in my face after I left home, feeling I abandoned her? She knew that also had penetrated inside me much further in the past few months – especially when I knew that my mother was dying. Even though I'd reconciled some of the guilt I had over leaving her after my mother found peace with Kathy, not all of it left me. Some things never do when you learn them when you're only a child.

We sat in her room for a few hours. There was no way we could be anywhere else and let go of the little time remaining with her. We knew the end was probably near. Then Kathy looked at me and finally asked me a question. But I didn't know if there was a good answer.

"Should I stay or would you like me to leave?

"Will you stay for at least a little while longer?" I replied. "Or as long as you can."

"Yes, I will, Bobby," Kathy said.

I didn't know what was best, to be alone or not – though I was certain it was my mother's last few hours. How could I not want the person who did so much for my mother to stay with me? Kathy had done what no one else might have done for her. Someone who put aside the unforgettable hatred between them, giving my mother some life while confronting death. Her last few months had been filled with compassion and grace, to now die with a little dignity.

I knew that Kathy would have preferred to leave after staying with me for a few hours. As much as she had done for my mother, it was intolerable for her to watch people get as sick as my mother – lying unconscious, just bones, and her last breath probably not being much longer. She had done what was needed for her. But as tough as she was on the outside, she didn't have enough strength to see someone suffer, especially seeing what my mother had gone through.

The doctors told us at first they weren't certain if my mother had a few hours left, a day, or a little longer. But after a while, they had more of a feeling she would die at some point in the night. I wanted her to go quickly, not to suffer more than she had been, but also to spare me the pain of some of the guilt that I still felt for not seeing her again until it was too late. It was probably selfish even to think of myself and not have more compassion for her fate. But I couldn't live the way I had anymore. I needed the guilt that still lingered to end after she died.

Kathy stayed with me in my mother's room for a little while longer to further discuss the funeral plans. She also asked me how long I would stay with my mother. I told her that I wouldn't leave until she was no longer here. I had to know that I didn't forget my mother, even if I had in many ways, probably for far too long. Kathy didn't say much after what I said, but she told me that I was doing what had to be done.

I turned to my stepmother and looked at her, feeling such an inner peace with how her and my mother had reconciled before it was too late. As what I felt became even far more meaningful, I subtly leaned over to Kathy's chair. What I could never tell her before couldn't wait any longer.

> "I've needed to say thank you for longer than you'll ever know, after everything you've done for me. You know that I couldn't have done what you did for me – helping me leave home to survive and find a future, and everything that you've done for my mother."

> "No one else would have done what you did."

> "I didn't know if you knew why I could never tell you until now?"

She replied and said:

> "I know your mother always had such control over both of her children's minds. She always hated me and thought of me as her enemy – a German Deichke, who stole your father from her and his kids."

> "That was your mother. She poisoned both of you. I'm just glad that she finally was able to see me a little differently."

I responded by saying:

> "Yes, there were some very bitter things that were even often hard to hear she said about you for many years. But there was no way for us to feel differently. We were children and could only believe what she was telling us."

We didn't say anything more. I knew that my mother had done most of what Kathy said. But I wished that she would have remembered what she said to my mother when she reconciled with Kathy. After what my mother told her, she voiced more kindness than I'd ever heard even after she knew my mother was dying.

I felt it was a real understanding for everything she had gone through from the inhumanity of her past. But for whatever reason, she didn't know that it impacted her the way it did, in the hatred for her and all Germans. As I'd said, even if time might have healed some of her trauma after the Holocaust, it had to have been triggered again, when my father left her being pregnant for a German woman.

The things she said about my mother, while often true, were still that painfully hard to hear. But after what happened between them for more than two decades, how would every bit of my stepmother's hatred just go away? It must not have been enough that my mother had reconciled with her.

Whatever resentment was left probably wouldn't let her forget how far my mother pushed my brother and I against her. I honestly wasn't surprised that Kathy hadn't said anything different. But I had to remember my mother for who she was when she reconciled with my stepmother. Even if it would be only temporary, I had to leave behind the trauma that followed me when I was growing up. Otherwise, I wouldn't have been able to remain near my mother's bedside in her final hours.

It was getting near 6:00 and Kathy told me that she wanted to tell my father how my mother was doing and when she'd be home. I didn't know if it mattered to him that she wanted to be with me and my mother in the remaining hours before she died. But he didn't encourage her to be there – especially since he felt betrayed by everything she was doing, knowing his feelings for her.

I knew my father also couldn't get past how Kathy could have done what she did for her, knowing how much they despised each other.

Still, despite what he felt, it really bothered me that he wouldn't come to the hospital. But I knew that if he didn't see my mother when he and Kathy came to my mother's house a few weeks ago, he wouldn't now.

If my father couldn't come to see her before she died, out of a little compassion for her, could he at least have done it for me? But he probably couldn't move past resenting my mother much, feeling my mother forced him to be with her against his will. Still I guess parents often can't see when they destroy each other in a marriage and maybe worse if they get divorced, how much it can impact their children.

When Kathy called him, I was pretty surprised the first words he said to her were to ask how my mother was doing. Considering how he felt, I didn't know why he even asked. But maybe it was to only see whether she had died.

Kathy replied by saying:

> "She doesn't have much time left. There is gornisht left of her now. Are you home?"

"Yes, but tell me what time you're coming home", he said.

> "Maybe in an hour. You know we have all the arrangements for her funeral. She'll be buried in Westlawn, very near your mother, Moishe, in the "Carnation" section. It was her wish."

> "The funeral will be within a day of when she dies. I guess maybe Thursday, if she passes away later this evening. Moishe, you know in the Jewish religion, a person's funeral is no longer than 24 hours after someone dies."

"Yes, I know," he said.

> "I am just glad she has us to be there for her now. She has no one else. But you know Harry can't come to the funeral. He almost became violent when he recently came over to see Rose. He wouldn't leave until we told him that we'd call the police if he didn't go."

> "Bobby will tell Harry after the funeral that his mother passed away. Hopefully he'll understand what he tells him, even with his illness."

> "I know he won't leave here until she passes away. He told me he'll stay with her."

My father really didn't say much after what Kathy said. I hoped that he'd say more, like he cared a little, but it wasn't surprising that he didn't. I don't know why it mattered to me, except being my father, he could have at least consoled me a little, knowing I was losing my mother. But he had to feel a marriage that my grandmother and not my mother likely forced him into was a prison sentence. He probably never loved my mother or wanted to be with her. The time they were together only built upon his feelings. Still, I had a hard time accepting how little he cared about her, especially now. But I wasn't him an couldn't understand things from his perspective.

Every bit of my mother's hatred for Kathy over my lifetime wasn't due to the person she was that made my stepmother reciprocate. But as I've said, they were only perceptions that were never true for all Germans by the trauma that came from what she lived through in the Holocaust. Maybe that's why Kathy found some of the compassion for her when she was dying that my father never could. He and my mother never would have reconciled like she and probably Kathy had done in some ways.

I sat for a little while longer with my stepmother and then said goodbye to her.

> "Kathy, I know you can't stay here any longer. You can't see her like this anymore. It has to be affecting you."

> "I know you're not able to watch people suffer like she did. But I told you that I have to stay with her until the end. But I'll go, if I can't be here any longer."

> "Thank you again for being here with me and what you've done for my mother. I can never tell you enough that I wouldn't have been able to go through this with her, if you hadn't been there."

She replied and said:

> "I know. You know me a little, how could I not help take care of her and be here now? She had no one else, except you, but you're still young and have never gone through this before."

> "It's just the way that I've always been. Even if your father thought I was a little crazy for what I did, I just had to be there for her. I saw how much she really needed me."

After she left, I picked up my chair from the end of the bed and moved it next to my mother. The chair was touching the front of the bed where she was lying. I grabbed her right hand. It was just thin strands of bones covered by yellow skin. I held it for a while, watching her resting comfortably. I felt at such peace being with my mother after she reconciled with Kathy. How much that had lifted some of the heavy weight of feeling that I abandoned my mother when I left home. But I remained cautious that those feelings would last, until that was finally put to rest on Yom Kippur Day in 1993.

In my mother's remaining hours, my mind turned to some memories that were centered around her when I was growing up. I remembered the good and bad things from back then. She made certain that when Harry went out with his friends, despite him being ten years older and probably not wanting his kid brother around, that I was sometimes included. It meant so much to me growing up – thinking it was so cool for a young kid to be with their older brother and his friends.

I've said that I was a very spoiled kid by my father, which I felt was partially to "buy my love" since he wasn't around much. But I'd also told, it was more to help resolve his guilt for leaving my mother. Without him around, my mother and brother disciplined me, and some of her punishment was pretty extreme.

When I was a kid, I often stole money from my mother's purse or stayed out with my friends far longer than when she wanted. Or I'd cry for hours, if I didn't get the junk food I wanted or my favorite toy. Her punishment was telling me that I had to go to the basement of our two flat building. It was what you might expect, very dark when the lights weren't on, many things in storage spaces, a washer and dryer, and the pipes and furnaces for the building. Everything you touched down there was covered with dust and dirt on the surfaces.

When I had to go downstairs, she turned off all the lights and locked the door nearly every time. I couldn't come back upstairs for at least two hours. There wasn't even a place to sit down. It was no way to punish a child, even if I was that bad. It was the only thing besides her stories of the Holocaust that terrified me and gave me nightmares. I often even thought there was a monster down there. He was the "boogey man," and I always couldn't have been more afraid that he'd kill me first and then my family.

It was near 8:00 and I was getting really tired and hungry. My mother was still breathing but even slower than before. She was still gently resting in a peaceful coma – leaving behind nearly three months of unrelenting pain. Nothing was left of her, except bones covered in the blue robe she loved. I just couldn't leave, especially now during probably her last hour or two.

By staying, it was the only way to resolve some of what I felt by not seeing her for that long. Maybe it would have been better for Kathy to stay with me until the end. But I was no longer afraid of being alone with my mother, feeling less of the guilt that sometimes overcame me after I left home. I also was no longer victimized by mother's dark perceptions of my stepmother that had stayed with me since childhood. I could finally accept her for who she was and not feel that I betrayed her by my relationship with Kathy. There was every bit of hope that I would fully reconcile from my past.

I couldn't stop noticing how hungry I was after not having eaten all day. But I convinced myself not to eat, since I felt it would interrupt everything that I needed to feel as my mother's time was ending. I told myself that I wanted my emotions to be as raw as possible and food would get in the way. While I wanted to leave and go eat, I couldn't, knowing that she would have wanted me to stay. How could I not honor her wishes, now that she had finally let me know her like I hadn't before? Both of us were no longer traumatized, thanks to the peace she found in letting go of her hatred for my stepmother.

As I sat next to her, holding her hand, feeling her fingers that were so fragile it was almost like they were cracking, I remembered being that needy as a child. I couldn't be home with a babysitter other than my brother. I'd even cry for 20 – 30 minutes after my mother dropped me off at school until I was maybe 10 or 11. One night, my mother left me at home with the only babysitter I probably I ever had. Her name was Karen. My mother had gone to a dance. Once she left, I was crying hysterically in front of Karen.

> "When is my mother coming home? I want her to come home now. Where is she? I can't be home without her, or at least my brother. You have to find her or my brother and tell them one of them has to come back here."

Karen didn't do much except tried to calm me down for a little while. But that didn't work. She finally told me that she would see if my mother left a number where she was going, call and tell her it was an emergency. We both didn't know where my brother had gone that night. After Karen went into another room for a minute, I remembered my mother had gone to a Jewish dance held by The Laor Organization.

Karen probably wouldn't have been able to find a phone number for the dance hall, since Laor held events at many different locations in West Rogers Park and the north suburbs. They were a Jewish organization for European Jewish refugees from World II, who were Holocaust survivors. My mother would only really associate with Greenhorns (Yiddish word meaning "European refugees").

Finally, I couldn't take it anymore being home without my mother. While Karen was in another room, I snuck out of the house. When I left, I rushed out, I didn't want her to catch me before I'd gone. I was wearing only a pretty light jacket on a bitterly cold night in January. There was no time to find anything else. I'd remembered that my mother walked to the dance not being too far away, and she told me the building where it was being held. I ran and cried relentlessly probably for six blocks – all the way to where the dance was held.

When I came into the building, I was panting, breathing far too heavily from running that much on a freezing night. After I caught my breath, I also began shivering due to how cold it was that night. I went inside the building, ran up and down the stairs, moving frantically from one room to the next to find my mother.

There were several dances being held that night in the building and when I couldn't find where she was after 15 minutes, I really panicked. Finally, as I was just walking and crying, yelling "Where are you, Mom?" I found her in one of the spacious dance halls near the back of the building. She was sitting in the room by one of the tables talking with her friends. I ran over, stood next to her table and looked at her. There were tears pouring down every bit of my face.

"When are you coming home?" I cried hysterically. "I want you to come home. Harry is out somewhere, and I can't be alone. Why did you leave me home with a babysitter?"

She replied and said:

> "Why can't Karen take care of you? You're not alone. She's staying with you until I come home."

I replied by saying:

> "I can't be home alone without you or Harry. It really doesn't
> matter if she's home with me, while you're both gone. You
> know that I've never able to stay home without either of you,
> especially at night."

I know that my mother was certainly embarrassed, being there
with her friends, with her son crying in front of everyone like someone
was murdering him. She knew that she couldn't stay there with me
and grabbed me by the hand, which felt pretty viciously. We came
home, and at first was really upset. She asked me how I could run
away from home like that, especially at night. And she pointed at me
like she did when I was growing up, planning to punish me, saying,
"I felt pretty embarrassed by what you did in front of my friends You
have to learn not to do this again. Don't you want me to have a life and
some fun once in a while?"

But not long after what she said, I was comforted by her more than
I ever knew.

> "It's okay, it's okay. I'm here and will take care of you Bobby,
> as I always have. You're my shana yingele."

I felt that I only remembered the story now in my mother's last hours
– knowing despite the importance of your parents being there for you in
times of need, her overbearing affection was a means to keep me by her
side. I've said it was also the trauma of Holocaust survivors manifested
in overprotection of their children being that common, hearing the
stories of how the Nazis separated families, murdered children and any
others that couldn't work before everyone else. But I will never forget
that my mother never wanted me to leave her. Still could anyone really
blame her, being able to act differently – knowing what she lost in the
Holocaust. It had to have made everything even much worse by how
my father left her.

By all the loneliness my mother had lived with in life, I felt pretty
certain it was the only reason I was born. It didn't matter that she had
gone through four miscarriages. She needed another child. I'd said
my brother was 10 years older than me. Once he became an adult, she
knew I would still be home for many years. But once I left, I've told that
I slowly began to detach from her. Despite that she never wanted me
to leave home and raised me to be that dependent on her, I needed to
remember I was no longer that little boy who always needed his mother
and could continue to stand on my own when she died.

After finally seeing her in a different way than I had before, there was still a part of me that felt I wouldn't be able to control how much I'd miss her. Still knowing that I had lived on my own and taken care of myself, I felt that I could move forward with my life. How I could never be alone growing up due to her overprotecting me, let me see later in life that what she did was far more for her than for me. I just wished that I could have seen that more when I was getting a older.

The clock had reached near midnight when my stepmother called my mother's room. I answered after the phone rang three or four times. After having been there since just after 3:00 in the afternoon, I had fallen asleep in the past hour. I was that tired, having been there that long and didn't wake up until I heard the phone ring.

"How is she? Are you all right?"

I answered and said:

> "She's the same as before. She's resting like she deserves. I'm very hungry and tired.

"Why don't you leave?" she said.

> "I can't."

Kathy responded by saying:

> "You have to leave, get some rest and be ready for her funeral within the next day. The doctors told you when I was there, they feel she'd pass away tonight or early next morning."

"Maybe if nothing happens in the next hour, I'll finally leave. But I don't want to," I said.

"Please go, you've done enough," she said.

I didn't say anything more. I ate a Snickers bar when I woke up, since my hunger was all I could feel now. I looked over at my mother, as I continued sitting next to the front of the bed, holding her hand. She was just breathing so calmly, but the time in between each breath was much longer than in the past hour. I could barely even tell she was alive. Before she died, I had to say a few things to her that I would have wanted her to know.

> "Mom, I'm really happy you made Shimmas with Kathy. I know you also must feel some peace from that much hatred for her you could never let go. I'll do everything I can to always try and understand why."

"But how you felt about her were for the wrong reasons."

"I will miss you and I'm sorry I left home, but I had to go. Otherwise, I don't know what might have become of me. I was too afraid that I wouldn't have become any different than Harry. Maybe after you made peace with Kathy you understand what I had to do."

"I also couldn't live any longer with your hatred and trauma that I felt since I was a kid. But I know that you did what you could for me. Please know I will remember you did your best."

"I'll make sure Harry will be taken care for the rest of his life. I know that was one of your wishes. He'll be provided for when he needs things by what you left us. Please take care. I love you. Goodbye, Mom."

I stayed until 1:30 in the morning, sitting silently next to the bed, with what remained of her – knowing I just couldn't be there any longer. In addition to the hunger and how tired I was after more than 12 hours, I just didn't want to feel any more memories of how I grew up. I couldn't do that any longer. It was too painful of a time in my life. I had to know that I had done everything I could, even if it wasn't until I knew that my mother was probably dying.

My mother died at 4:30 that morning, a few hours after I left. When the hospital called to tell me that she passed away, I just remembered the moment her and my stepmother had finally made Shimmas. How could I think of anything else, except how in the Midst of Darkness, she had reconciled with Kathy?

I called Kathy to tell her my mother had died. She just said:

"I'm very sorry that you've lost her. She told me how much she cared about you, and I told her why you had to leave home. You couldn't be around her trauma and what that was doing to you."

I also had to tell her, how afraid you were that you'd wind up like Harry, if you stayed. She didn't say much when I told her that. Maybe it was just too hard for her to hear – knowing it was the truth."

As I've said, it felt Kathy didn't really want to be there for my mother when she first saw her, even knowing she was dying. After I pleaded for her help, it also didn't appear to change her feelings. She must have looked at my mother and finally realized how much she was suffering, knowing I couldn't be her being her caretaker.

My mother's reconciliation with Kathy, after what she did for her, I've always felt had to have saved my mother before she died. Maybe it would save her soul, give her peace of mind, or just let her know that she'd finally done the right thing. Oskar Schindler did as well, when he crossed over the line standing between inhumanity and humanity – saving more than 1200 Jewish lives, including my mother's in the midst of darkness.

It was October 1993, and I was with my father and Kathy at Ezras Israel Synagogue in West Rogers Park on Yom Kippur Day. Rabbi Schwartzman was delivering the morning sermon, the story of a German industrialist and member of the Nazi Party – Oskar Schindler. He told how Schindler had saved over 1200 Jewish people during the Holocaust by employing them in his enamelware and ammunitions factories in Nazi-occupied Poland (Plaszow) and Brunnlitz, Czechoslovakia. The story the Rabbi told that day was due to the movie *Schindler's List* being released next month.

I listened to only part of the Rabbi's speech, being asleep when he first began talking. My stamina wasn't too good, having to fast all day and standing frequently for many prayers, not to mention the length of Rabbis' sermons on Yom Kippur day. But when I opened my eyes, listening to what the Rabbi was saying, I couldn't stop listening. It couldn't have been a more powerful and moving story. But I questioned how this man could be the humanitarian he was amongst a Fascist power of terror and the mesmerizing numbers of those who had been the unconscionable supporters of Nazi ideology. That many who were complicit in the "Final Solution" – the Jewish Genocide.

As the Rabbi's speech ended and my stepmother was sitting on the other side of my father, he leaned over and said six words to me that I would never forget. It was five years after my mother passed away, and he told me something that she never did. They were six words I would never forget.

"Your mother was on that list."

In synagogue that day, 40% of the congregation were Holocaust survivors. Some I knew personally from having lived in West Rogers Park growing up. I can't even imagine what they might have been feeling, hearing in their synagogue the first major story of the Holocaust that Steven Spielberg had also turned into a movie. Most importantly, it was a story of a Nazi German saving Jewish lives.

A person who turned righteous when so few did, within the darkest period of history. If some of those survivors might have been like my mother, who were traumatized and hated all Germans, could hearing this story have changed anything for them? I have to believe it might have reconciled at least some of what they felt. How could it not?

My mother had told me several times what she knew of her parents four sisters and a brother, who were murdered in the gas chambers of the Belzec and Auschwitz death camps. I also listened to the atrocities she lived through in the Plaszow concentration camp led for a while by the Butcher of Plaszow – Amon Goeth. I also remembered the fear she lived with for the month she was in Auschwitz. But I never really understood why she never told me that Oskar Schindler had saved her and every other Jewish life he could from the fate of 6 million other Jews in the Holocaust.

She was in Auschwitz for a month in October, 1944 when Schindler finally arranged for her transfer, and that of 299 other women to his new factory in Brunnlitz, Czechloslovakia. He actually did that while in jail, when it was discovered that he was bribing the Gestapo. The bribes were too overlook favorable treatment that he was giving to his Jewish workers.

The Nazis had mistakenly transferred the women to Auschwitz, from Schindler's Emalia factory in Plaszow. While she was there for only a month, I can't even begin to imagine the panic she must've felt once the gates opened and she entered the camp. My mother must have been in shock knowing that she had family who died there, being murdered in the gas chambers. How could she not feel that this would also be her fate?

The meaning of Schindler saving her life would never be more unmeasurable than when she was in Auschwitz. Her death was inevitable after she knew what happened to her family. In some ways, I felt what Schindler did parallels another defining moment for my mother before she died. She finally had seen that Kathy had given her life confronting death. She was still going to die, but the peace inside herself she had to have found after the lifetime of hatred for my stepmother probably did save her soul. Schindler had also rescued her when her fate was never more certain than in Auschwitz.

After learning my mother was a "Schindler" Jew on Yom Kippur Day, right before the movie was released, I've felt was one of the two greatest blessings from God. The other was the day my mother made Shimmas with Kathy.

Yom Kippur for Jewish people is the holiest day of the year, committing them to a reconciliation of the heart and forgiveness of their sins. It's that final redemption I found after the lifetime of hatred for my stepmother and every other German, knowing my mother was saved by Oskar Schindler and Kathy. How much more could that have meant for me, to put to rest any hatred for my stepmother? It let me find a permanent reconciliation of my feelings for her, to finally forget every bit of my mother's vengeance for my stepmother that penetrated too far inside me.

After hearing many stories of everything she went through, being traumatized after unconscionable darkness, how could my mother and I have felt differently about all Germans? But Yom Kippur Day ended any hate that was left not only for Kathy, but all Germans. It was done by the only way it could have been – getting me to see "people as people." Why wouldn't I, after hearing that a Nazi risked his life and lost everything he had to save my mother and every other Jewish life he could? It's the compassion that we must have for each other, knowing that we can be different but still look at each other the same.

The defining moment of reconciliation I found for Kathy a few weeks before my mother died, that became permanent on Yom Kippur Day has let me aspire to what I've become. Someone with understanding, openness and objectivity who wants to do everything possible to have my own lens for how I see others – free from the way I grew up, with inherited trauma manifested in unjust hatred.

But mostly, I've opened myself to what I could have never done before. The learning by my past resting in never losing hope that even in the midst of darkness we can still overcome what pulls us apart. It's what Oskar Schindler did for my mother and so many other Jewish lives he saved that no one else would. It's also I've felt what my stepmother had done for her. How could anyone not want their conviction to compassion – the way they found humanity standing in the eyes of inhumanity?

The Shoah Foundation, established in 1994, founded by Steven Spielberg – only one year after Schindler's List was released, which he directed – is dedicated to the testimonials of survivors and witnesses of the Holocaust. It was the voice my mother never had. I know how incredibly meaningful it would have been for her to tell her story there for many others to hear. How much more could that have meant to her, being a Schindler's List survivor?

If she could have told the story of her teenage life as a Schindler Jew, would it have changed any of her bitterness for my stepmother, before she finally reconciled with her right before she died? I feel it can't be said enough that her life as a Schindler survivor must have been deeply buried and probably forgotten after my father left her. But I felt that she also never told the full story of her life in the Holocaust due to not having the right of passage for testimony.

The Shoah Foundation has given that voice to over 59,000 Holocaust survivors since it was established in 1994, five years after my mother passed away. The foundation and its right of passage for survivors to tell what happened to them in the Holocaust would have meant everything to her. The voice that my mother never had has meant so much for Jews and non-Jews across the world for the past 30 years. Those who have been the survivors of a genocide.

Stories of "Second Generation" ("2G") Survivors – Confronting Their Parent's Holocaust Survivor Trauma

The stories being told are interviews of three people – one who wanted to remain anonymous, that were inflicted with Second Generation survivor trauma. Their trauma like for me and my brother began as children. Each of the 2G survivor's inherited trauma affected them in different ways. These stories were included as a supplement to the memoir for letting those who don't know and reminding everyone else both how trauma can begin and the potential gravity of the impact, if not treated or treated improperly.

The Holocaust being probably one of the darkest periods in history left survivor's with trauma that genetically as research has discovered subsequent generations have had to bear. Of no less importance, something that monumental of horror intuitively has to be trauma that survivors in some way passed onto their children, which their children's children have probably inherited, at least to some extent and maybe the next generation(s) to come.

Child of a Holocaust survivor – The father was in many concentration camps, including Auschwitz, Mauthausen and Theresienstadt. While the mother was in two concentration camps – Auschwitz and Bergen-Belsen. The father never discussed much with his child about what he went through in the camps. But his mothered shared everything with the child, which began not even yet celebrating a fifth birthday, telling what she went through in the Holocaust. The child's "Second Generation" holocaust trauma was due to the mother's trauma.

In Auschwitz, the mother lived in better conditions than many other Jews and the others who were incarcerated in the concentration camp. Her more favorable treatment was due to playing the mandolin in the Auschwitz women's orchestra. The Nazis' had official orchestras in the concentration camps to exploit music and deceive the prisoners, letting them feel that after a 20-hour work day, their life wasn't that bad living in a concentration, or death camp.

The mother was eventually transferred from Auschwitz to the Bergen-Belsen concentration camp in northern German, where she was liberated. In the summer of 1944, the liquidation of Auschwitz began, as the Soviet army's offensive advanced into Eastern Europe and was moving into occupied Poland. The liquidation of Auschwitz was to hide evidence of the war crimes the Nazi's committed. If the Soviet Army had discovered the camp and the atrocities being committed their, the Nazis realized the would be held accountable for the terror inflicted on prisoners there.

As a result of the overcrowded and horrific living conditions in Bergen-Belsen, where disease and starvation flourished, hundreds of thousands of people, who were imprisoned their died. Anne Frank and some of her family also were deported to Bergen-Belsen. She died there due to starvation and typhoid.

The 2G survivor's mother was heavily impacted by trauma after what happened to her in the Holocaust. She wasn't able to have children for 14 years after she left Bergen-Belsen due to the famine and disease she was exposed to that manifested over every bit of the camp. The trauma maybe even began as a child being only two years old, hearing something the mother said that would never be forgotten – "I will never let you starve," Her obsession with food that came from her trauma due to some of her life in the Holocaust – fighting to exist in a starvation camp, became the origin of the 2G trauma inherited from the mother.

The mother would literally take food out of her mouth that she would partially chew and give it to her child, who was just two or three. I was told that she often mentioned, "you have to eat everything I give you." You don't where your next meal will come from." The trauma passed onto him from the mother led to being extremely overweight, which began in grade school and has never been different throughout adult life. Today, being an adult, standing at 5'11 since being 16 has never weighed less than 350 lbs.

Whenever there was food in front of the child growing up, and as an adult, it has to be eaten. I was told, there is sometimes even panic, if not known when is the next meal to be eating again.

One time, the mother demanded that her child go on a diet being that overweight. But she would still make food, leave the kitchen and then watch in the next room, if the food had been eaten.

The mother also used to dress and shower the child growing up until being 12, or 13. She would also walk her child to school until that age. In grade school, there was relentless bullying inflicted by other kids to the child due to being overweight and taken to school until becoming an older kid. The bullying also traumatized the child and led to becoming even becoming far heavier into adult life.

As I've told in the chapters, after the Holocaust it's been common for survivors to overprotect their children. The trauma is manifested reflexively like most forms. It's purely survivors' reaction to the unconscionable things the Nazi's senselessly did, no more so than to Jewish people, including repeatedly separating children from their parents and older brothers and sisters. It's what happened to my mother, except she didn't die like that many other kids, being saved by Oskar Schindler.

Fortunately in grade school, the child had seen a therapist for 2G trauma. But in high school, as a teenager couldn't help but rebel against the mother for the trauma she inflicted. She was beaten up a couple times by her teenage kid. These attacks were due to blaming her for being forced to overeat and overprotected as a child. What the mother did resulted in embarrassing him and being bullied by kids in class, especially being far too heavy for a kid his age.

As an adult, the 2G survivor has not been very transparent having three children that have been raised not telling them everything his mother had done. They haven't been told much to protect the kids from confronting the baggage of the penetration of trauma the mother had as a survivor, that was passed on to her child.

Daphna Boros – Born in Israel to Holocaust survivors, raised in America, – I don't recall when I first realized that my parents carried a secret burden of suffering. I also don't remember when they first told me about their painful quests for survival. They delivered their accounts differently. My father's account was laden with anger and resentment.

He spoke eloquently – elegantly – in almost baroque cadences. What he described was inconceivable. A father who disappeared not once – but twice – into Prisoner of War camps. A mother and infant brother who relied on him – a 12-year old – to secretly leave their Budapest ghetto and scrounge for food. A note of pride would emerge whenever he spoke of his resourcefulness in looting an abandoned factory – right under the noses of Ukrainian soldiers - and returning home with life-sustaining loaves of bread. Repeatedly, he told me of the time, when he was a teenager that him and a few of his friends were wrenched from their ghetto cellars and lined up against the wall – ready to be executed until a petty power struggle between authoritarian monsters saved them from certain death.

In contrast, my mother's telling was dispassionate. Her matter of fact tone seemed almost detached from the horrors she described. Her parents and older brother were taken away to concentration camps, where they perished. She miraculously survived a period of hiding through her parents' advance planning, her own wits, and the charity of a few righteous Gentiles. As a pre-teen, she fled through forests dotted with Partisan soldiers, slept in ditches, hopped on trains riddled with Nazi soldiers, and somehow arrived back in Bratislava - only to find that she was orphaned.

As if that pain wasn't devastating enough, she had contracted scarlet fever and was isolated in quarantine – with no one to comfort or hold her. That last scene haunts me more than any other my parents described. To this day, I feel a surge of angry protectiveness when I think of the doctors and nurses who quarantined her. While other children dreamed of magical wishes that would bring gold coins and big houses, I dreamed of the opportunity to go back in time and be near my mother at that very moment, comforting her with my love in some fantastical, generation-swapping miracle.

Perhaps unsurprisingly, my own earliest memories were of being chased and my childhood dreams were all nightmares. They were my parent's nightmares that became my nightmares. From infancy until age four - leaving home, walking down a driveway, lying in the dark – all required dedicated assistance from my parents and my older sister (whose envied confidence stood in stark contrast to my timidity).

When I was eight, we left the relative safety of our diverse neighborhood, and moved to a homogeneous "all American" suburb.

It was then that I started to feel a compelling instinct to protect my parents. From what, exactly? I cannot say. Initially from the xenophobic reception of our neighbors. Also from the condescending reaction of doctors and teachers, who responded to my mother's thick accent and hearing loss as one would to a child. Honestly, anyone in a position of authority would get into my cross-hairs.

Rather strangely, I began insisting on accompanying my mother to her appointments. If I sensed even a moment of disrespect, I would cast aside my previous shyness and glare. If that didn't right the perceived wrong, I would deliver a stinging verbal corrective. This wasn't just unusual coming from a little girl – it must have been perceived as grossly inappropriate. I didn't care. I was still insecure about my own place in the world. But when it came to my parents – I was fearless to the point of being offensives.

When I think back on those years, I initially feel a spark of shame. But soon that old familiar sense of indignation begins to course through my veins again. It's as if all of my rage against the inhumanity of the Nazis and their collaborators got funneled against some poor unsuspecting physician. This guard dog mentality didn't wane as I aged. If anything, my compulsion to speak out against any perceived injustice spread. I worked with juvenile delinquents in college and enrolled in Harvard Law School with the plan to save the souls of young offenders. But at no time in my life was I ever more vigilant than I was as a child – reacting with fierce urgency to anyone who threatened my parents' dignity.

Along with this evident externalization, I began to develop a preternatural attunement. to my parents' moods. A downcast look or faraway glance was enough to spark intense worry on my part. Why were my parents sad? The next immediate thought was – how can I heal them? I knew something outside of my control was responsible for my parents' sorrow. I didn't feel responsible for their pain. But I felt wholly responsible for healing it. This is how my 2G trauma has manifested itself ever since.

When I sense anyone in psychic pain – my parents, my children, my students, even my dog – I feel an urgent, or need to dispel it. I do this often at the expense of my own mental wellbeing. I exhaust myself overprotecting them – offering assistance, consolation, approbation, reassurance – anything to turn the tide and bring them back to safety. I have wondered how my smothering affection at times for my children may impact them as they grow older. Will they be able to stand on their own – not be able to take care of themselves, or far worse pass on how my 2G trauma manifested to their children.

It took me decades to understand that this perplexing reaction (some would call it a martyr's complex) had anything to do with my parents' wartime trauma. Indeed, it wasn't until my 50's, when my niece – a librarian's assistant at Columbia University – happened to check out a Holocaust-themed book to a woman by the name of Dr. Irit Felsen. On her recommendation, I began reading Felsen's article, entitled "Our Parents, Ourselves, Our Changing Lives: Summaries of lectures 1-9 from the meeting series for the Bikur Cholim Chesed Organization, 2016-2017. This one publication changed my understanding of my parents and of myself.

I still react with inappropriate indignation at authority figures. It is a running joke with my colleagues, who marvel at the level of hostility I expel at any perceived, maybe even misunderstood feeling of authoritarianism. But it has cost me. Refusing to " be nice" to the bosses caused them to pass over me for promotions and bonuses. I don't care much. It seems to me a small price to pay compared to the inexpressible suffering my parents went through. I wish I could have protected them from pain. Then I wished I could have healed them. Barring that, I guess I'll continue to rail against perceived tyrants – or really anyone wearing a badge or standing in my loved ones' path.

Liz – She is the daughter of a father, who was a Holocaust survivor. He was in the Stuttof and Dachau concentration camps. Liz's father also was held in the Shauli Ghetto of Lithuania until it was liberated. The Holocaust left him with the fear of money due to the Nazi's selflessly taken everything which his family owned and the trauma of his past.

But he didn't tell her or the rest of his family much of the atrocities that traumatized him during the Holocaust, or the family he lost. Still, his trauma became Liz's when she was a child, not even yet celebrating her 10th birthday. She inherited his fear of money, but the major traumatic obsession that never left her was how she felt responsible for everything he went through. She always thought the worst of everything, knowing her father was a Holocaust survivor.

Liz could never really confront her pain due to her inherited trauma. She never really told her family that she was bearing every bit of her father's suffering. While she had a Bachelor's degree that was from a top college, The University of Michigan and a Masters of Fine Arts, she never really consistently held a job after finishing her studies. Her anxiety and fear that she inherited from her father just often left her debilitated, trapped with anxiety and unable to function.

When she reached her 40's unable to detach from the trauma of her father's past, not having a family or a career, she suppressed her unstable emotions with anxiety medication. The book she also compiled of her father's story, when finally hearing everything he'd been through, giving testimony to the Shoah Foundation, made his trauma penetrate her that much more. She finally heard some of the atrocities that he saw or might have been subjected to during the Holocaust.

After Liz could no longer detach from her feelings, she needed heavier doses of pills that eventually reached uncontrollable levels to cope with her suffering left by debilitating anxiety manifested in emotional instability that was aggressively climbing. She had finally become an addict of anti-depressants and anxiety medication in her mid to late 50's. After she turned 59, in mid-summer her addiction had reached a stage where she was in crisis. She was hoping to get help for her abuse of psychiatric drugs and had gone to two hospitals in the Chicago area to be admitted. The first one discharged her in less than a day.

They both had in-patient substance abuse programs. But one of the hospitals didn't have an in-patient program for abuse of psychiatric drugs. While the other one did have a psychiatric unit and treated this type of substance abuse. By not telling them that she was suicidal and without good insurance, that hospital admitted her, but as I said she was discharged in less than a day.

The second one didn't admit her, not having a substance abuse program for psychiatric drugs. She had told both of the hospital's patient's intake teams, "I look okay on the outside, but not on the inside." When they saw her purse filled with pills, they had to have known she was also over medicated, especially the way she talked and probably looked. They both released Liz, apparently not being stable. But couldn't the hospital with the substance abuse program she needed, seen her condition and not discharged her until it no longer seemed that she was in a crisis?

Her other sister, Marci heard what happened and that she needed help urgently. She found a substance abuse prevention program in Florida and was to be admitted in the next week after she had driven Liz from Chicago to her family's home in Detroit. Liz went to sleep that night and the next afternoon when her sister returned from work, she went into her room and when she'd seen that she wasn't moving shouted her name. She didn't answer, and finally after seeing that she wasn't breathing she knew she was dead. It was determined that she died from an overdose of psychiatric drugs that she'd been abusing for years.

Anita, one of her other two sisters, who had the same biological father as Liz also suffered from his trauma, but many years of behavioral therapy helped her function much better than Liz. It let her confront the trauma that Liz never could. As I have shared in the story overview and hopefully what's learned in the chapters of the memoir is "How We Can't Change the Behavior – Trauma, without awareness of the behavior.

Acknowledgments

In Memory of

This memoir is written in memory of the **11 million victims** sources have told (albeit potentiually understimated), who died in the Holocaust, that were murdered and dehumanized due to Nazi ideology that was manifested in racism. Of which, there were six million Jews who lost their lives in the Holocaust, including my mother's parents, four sisters and a brother, who were murdered in the gas chambers of Auschwitz and the Belzec extermination camps.

Secondly, I have written this story in memory of **my mother**, who died in 1988 due to colon cancer. Her death at 62 may have been prevented if detected earlier, but couldn't due to some of the ways that her Holocaust survivor trauma manifested. Trauma that heavily impacted my mother throughout her life and what she passed down to myself and my brother.

The memoir is also in memory of **my brother**, who passed away when he was 61 due to a lung disease living in a nursing home. He had been institutionalized for his mental illness after he was no longer able to care of himself before he was 30. I only hope this story will better help us see that 2G trauma, which penetrated him far more than me demands that we find ways to treat the trauma, before we can't. Otherwise, the unconscionable cost can be what happened to him.

Dedications

The story is firstly dedicated to every **Holocaust survivor**, who lives with the trauma of the atrocities they've remembered from that period. Some of their trauma has been discussed with their families or friends and sometimes not. But regardless, something that traumatic in life that people lived through, whether its visible or not can't be ignored.

Secondly, the memoir is dedicated to the **children of Holocaust survivors**, who have inherited their parents' trauma, the trauma also passed onto their children and what future generations may have to bear.

If we only consider, approximately 3.5 million European Jews who survived the Holocaust, and the 6.5 million who didn't, applying that same proportion for the non-Jewish survivors with the other at least five million victims, conservatively there may be 10-15 million direct descendants. Of which, there may be many of them, who are inflicted by the trauma of their parents. That also doesn't consider the grandchildren of survivors, or the trauma that may be passed on to future generations.

I have also dedicated the memoir to **my stepmother Kathy**. She returned to her family in Berlin in the late 1990's, a few years after my father passed away. We don't talk much anymore, but I will never forget what she did for me and my mother. I'm not too certain anyone else would have done what she did, putting aside the past to do what had to be done in the midst of darkness. The help that we needed, not able to help ourselves, trapped in a crisis.

This book is also dedicated to **my wife Jody Schneiderman**, who I have loved more than anyone. She was apprehensive at first for us traveling to Poland and visiting the Auschwitz and Plaszow concentration camps for part of our eighth anniversary – as one may expect. We visited the camps for research that was needed I've shared in the memoir. I always remember when I began writing the memoir she told me that she'd only be able to read the book after it was published. She wasn't ready yet to read everything that happened to me and my brother growing up that's been written in the memoir.

My wife has been far more than an inspiration, telling me to keep going and that "God's rejection is your protection," despite some of the literary agents I contacted that couldn't relate enough to the story. Many of them were far younger than me. I honestly feel they probably didn't grow up hearing their mother telling them everything that happened to her and her family in the Holocaust. My brother and I often listening to her nightmares of the inhumane atrocities committed by the Nazi's that terrorized her, let alone what it did to both of us.

There is no way I could tell **Oskar Schindler** what he did for the over 1248 Jewish lives he saved, including my mother. But hopefully, what I've told about the *Schindler's List* story will continue to let the world know that what he did could never be more meaningful, especially for the Schindler survivors and more than 8,000 descendants of Schindler Jews living now after that generation. What Schindler did also can't be more important learning since the Holocaust than today for **"how we can come together from what pulls us apart."**

This book could also never have been written if it wasn't for **Leopold Pfefferberg (Poldek)**. He was a Schindler survivor, who sat down with an author named Thomas Keneally in the back of his leather and repair shop in Beverly Hills in 1980 and told him the story of Oskar Schindler and *"Schindler's List."* When Poldek immigrated to the US after the Holocaust, he changed his last name to Page, which he felt would better assimilate his family to life in America. Mr. Keneally wrote the book – *"Schindler's Ark"* after Poldek told him the Schindler story.

The book was optioned to Universal Pictures and the screen play was turned into *Schindler's List*. The film is considered one of the most important movies ever made, that Steven Spielberg directed. If not for Poldek, I would have never known my mother was a Schindler's List survivor. I only wish that I would have the opportunity to sit down with Poldek and tell him the story of my mother's life in the memoir that I've written. He probably would have wanted to know that what he did couldn't have meant more to me.

Marie Knecht – Poldek's daughter has carried on her father's memory telling the story of everything he did when he came to America, honoring his promise to Oskar Schindler after the Holocaust – he would tell the story of his life and *Schindler's List*. She has shared the story for the past few years with synagogues, educational institutions, and recently began meeting with Holocaust Museums for hoping to tell her father's story. How he told the world of Oskar Schindler.

Marie and her husband Jeffrey have become dear friends of ours over the past few years. We came to one the talks of her father's story. The story was told in Valley Beth Shalom synagogue, which is in Encino, California.

This memoir honors **Thomas Keneally** being the author of the book – *Schindler's Ark* that the film *Schindler's List* was based upon. After Keneally heard Poldek's story, he told Poldek that he didn't believe he was the right person to tell the Schindler story. He told him after what he heard that he couldn't write the book being too young, not Jewish and a Priest. Poldek then looked at him and told him with every bit of conviction – "That's exactly why you should write the story." After what Poldek said, Keneally went back to his hotel that night, reviewed his notes and began to write *Schindler's Ark*.

Finally and of no less importance, the memoir is also a tribute to **Steven Spielberg** for directing the movie *Schindler's List*, which transformed America's understanding of the Holocaust, and brought the darkest period of history to the forefront of the public's consciousness. After Schindler's Ark was published in 1982 and Universal Pictures acquired the rights to the story, it wasn't until ten years later towards the end of 1992, he decided to move forward and begin production of the film. Spielberg felt that he hadn't been emotionally or creatively mature enough to undertake such a sensitive and pivotal story before that time.

The growth in antisemitism and Holocaust denial also led Spielberg in the 1990's to finally decide that he needed to do the film. Poldek was also instrumental in contacting him nearly weekly after *Schindler's Ark* was published – over that ten-year period until 1992. It helped lead to the decision for him to want the film to be made. Poldek often asked Spielberg, "When are you going to get beyond making movies about dinosaurs and little furry things?"

After *Schindler's List* was released, Spielberg founded the Shoah Foundation in 1994, a year after the film's debut. He used everything he made from the movie to build the Shoah Foundation. Spielberg fulfilled his vision for *Schindler's List* to monetize the film to fund the Shoah Foundation for survivor testimonial. He wanted that more than anything else after what happened in the Holocaust – the right of passage for survivors to tell their stories. The voice my mother never had, I'm certain would have meant everything to her.

Special Thanks

How can I also not give that much credit to the team that I've been fortunate enough to collaborate with that helped me finish this memoir that hopefully readers see as that important in our world today as I feel.

Aemilia Phillips – I wanted to first thank Aemilia Phillips, my editor, who has worked in the publishing industry the past nine years. She is a Harvard graduate and has been a literary agent with The Stuart Krichevsky Agency in New York. They are one of the top literary agencies in the country. When she began editing the first chapter or two, I didn't agree with some of her revisions. Her and I would argue when she encouraged me to not hold back on my emotions, especially being a memoir. She'd tell me don't ever be afraid to let readers know what your feeling, whether its expressed by words, silence or painting images of your emotions. I'd often tell her they'll know what I'm feeling, including every little detail of background for my family and the stories told. I just wanted to say one more time, thank you – from my heart for not letting me tell this story without sharing everything that I really felt.

David Ter-Avenyson – I would never be in the position I am to finish this memoir and tell the story the way it needs to be told without my book cover designer – David Ter-Avensyon / Ter33 Design. When I told him the story of the memoir he said that he had to be involved, and he has made my story more real than I ever felt was possible. The front book cover being the image of prisoners, who were Jewish women wearing headscarves behind the barbed wire in the Plaszow concentration camp and my mother's name and number seen on *Schindler's List*. The back cover picturing my mother's face in front of the black background of the list of Schindler survivors. The words under her picture telling how I learned Yom Kippur day, 1993 in synagogue, five years after my mother passed away, when the movie was being released my mother was a *Schindler's List* survivor.

Thank you again David for designing the book covers that hopefully will help readers, whether impacted by the Holocaust or not, about the story maybe a little the way I do, seeing even a bit of themselves, their parents, or their grandparents in some of what's been told. Whether impacted by the Holocaust or not, but confronting Intergenerational Trauma, or any bias that's been harmful, the story's ambition is to let us resonate with some of what's been told within the chapters.

Pierce Boydbagby and Sammy Rosensweig – Thank you both for all your efforts in helping me with this journey of telling this story to as many people as might be interested in reading the memoir I have written. Pierce is the principal of Boydbagby Digital Marketing. He and Sammy, who he's contracted for helping in marketing this book have designed my website for letting people know of the story that I've written and some insight for a better understanding of Intergenerational Trauma that hopefully turn into readers of the memoir. They've also coordinated other digital promotional services for developing public awareness and interest that hopefully let people decide they need to read the story.

Scott Moden – Thank you for everything you've done to bring my memoir into book form. Your work on the interior layout brought together all of the pieces of the manuscript. Your support with the cover files and the recommendation to include photographs were essential to turning my story into a finished publication that readers can relate to.

I can't say enough how much your comments meant to me when you first read what the story was about – not only the story of my mother who was a Schindler survivor, "but also a broader refection on the consequences of hatred and the path toward healing." I have to say your demeanor reminds me a little of Oskar Schindler.

Dr. Shana Franklin – She is a Harvard educated psychologist that was my former therapist. When I was seeing her towards the end of last year, I often told her that the story had to be perfectly written, otherwise it couldn't be told. I never would have finished writing this memoir if not for something she once told me, I'll never forget. "Don't perfect the story, just tell the story. Shana thank you, I really mean that. There's no way I could have written this story without often reminding myself of what you said. I'll always remember one other thing you told me – "What do you want to be remembered for?"

Mary Balise Nelligan – In December, 1993, when I began to write my first chapter of the book, we were invited to our dear friends, the Chambers' for their annual Christmas Brunch. I told Mary, who had been invited, the story of the memoir I began writing. What I mentioned to her, included learning from my father Yom Kippur day in synagogue my mother was a Schindler's List survivor – five years she passed away.

But for whatever reason, I had been reluctant to include what happened Yom Kippur day in the memoir, writing a story of Intergenerational Trauma and racial bias. Shockingly, I didn't feel that what I learned on Yom Kippur was that pivotal for a story of racism manifested in a lifetime of undeserved hatred. Mary, who is not Jewish, told me that's your story and don't write the memoir, if you don't tell what happened. How would I not listen to someone that's a prominent editor, who has written a book about her father's life.

Mary, thank you far more than I can say, for what you made me realize. The back book cover will let readers see how important what you told me is for this story.

Hirsch, Sali Hirschberg, Herz Hirschberg, Szymon Hirschberg,
witz, Roma Horowitz, Regina Horowitz, Bella Horowitz, Sara Horowitz,
eli, Izaak Izraelowicz, Salomon Jachzel, Abraham Jachzel, Jakób
Kahane, Felix Kamiński, Henryk Kammermann, Adela Karmel-Poss, Celina
ner, Eugen Kellner, Soltan Kellner, Szyja Kern, Estera Kerner, J
nberg, Bernard Kleiner, Meier Kleiner, Paula Kleinmann, Jakób
ler, Leo Knobloch, Chiel Kohane, Ruth Kohn, Markus Kohn, Awadie Koll
r, Henryk Kornfeld, Ludwik Kornfeld, Rozalia Kornhauser, Bernard Korn
ler, Helena Kühn, Jankiel Kujawski, Salo Kukurutz, Roman Kukuru
Jakób Langsam, Szaja Lasser, Róża Laufer, Jakób Laus, Ryszard Lax,
r, Abraham Lermer, Jakób Leser, Szulim Leser, Perla Leser, Jakób L
htig, Anna Lichtig, Ignacy Liebermann, Maurycy Liebermann, Salom
Ruth Löwenstein, Adela Löwi, Maria Löwi, Stefan Luftig, Leopold Luft
Massaryk, Abraham Matuschak, Kalman Meisels, Szlama Meisels, Józ
nderer, Rafał Morgenbesser, Adam Morgenbesser, Szymon Mowschowitz
el, Miklosz Nadler, Roma Nass, Hans Nebel, Dawid Neiger, Gizela Nes
sbaum, Henoch Nussbaum, Adolf Oberfeld, Kalman Obstler, Jakób Oestreic
r, Sara Peller, Hersch Pelzmann, Natan Pelzmann, Gusta Pelzmann,
Moses Perlmann, Jakób Perlmann, Ewa Perlmann, Izrael P

The wall of *Schindler's List* survivor's at the Emalia exhibit (Oskar Schindler's Enamel Factory); Historical Museum of Krakow Poland.

Róza Laufer: My mother's name, as it appears on the wall of survivors at the Emalia factory.

Leopold Pfefferberg (Poldek) standing next to
Oskar Schindler being seated.

Poldek, Thomas Keneally and Steven Spielberg (Left to Right) pictured at
a film premier for *Schindler's List*. It was a few weeks before the film was
officially released in December, 1993.

Oskar Schindler's grave in Mount Zion Cemetery, Jerusalem, Israel.

In Hebrew: THE RIGHTEOUS AMONG THE GENTILES.

In German: THE UNFORGETTABLE RESCUER OF 1200 PERSECUTED JEWS.